Juan and Marie Join the Class

Caught'ya! Grammar with a Giggle for Third Grade

verde   blanco   rojo

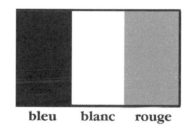

bleu   blanc   rouge

Jane Bell Kiester

Juan and Marie Join the Class
Caught'ya! Grammar with a Giggle for Third Grade

By Jane Bell Kiester

© 2007 Jane Bell Kiester
All rights reserved.

Cover design: David J. Dishman
Book design: Billie J. Hermansen
Editor: Emily Gorovsky

Library of Congress Cataloging-in-Publication Data

Kiester, Jane Bell, 1945-
  Juan and Marie join the class : Caught'ya! grammar with a giggle for third
grade / by Jane Bell Kiester.
      p. cm.
  Includes bibliographical references.
  ISBN-13: 978-0-929895-34-5 (pbk.)
  ISBN-10: 0-929895-34-7 (pbk.)
  1. English language—Grammar—Study and teaching (Primary) 2. Humor in
education. 3. Third grade (Education) I. Title.
  LB1528.K55 2006
  372.61—dc22
                                    2006012635

Also by Jane Bell Kiester
  Blowing Away the State Writing Assessment Test: Four Steps to Better Writing Scores for Students of All Levels
  Caught'ya! Grammar with a Giggle
  Caught'ya Again! More Grammar with a Giggle
  The Chortling Bard: Caught'ya! Grammar with a Giggle for High School
  Eggbert, the Ball, Bounces by Himself: Caught'ya! Grammar with a Giggle for First Grade
  Giggles in the Middle: Caught'ya! Grammar with a Giggle for Middle School
  Putrescent Petra Finds Friends: Caught'ya! Grammar with a Giggle for Second Grade

Maupin House publishes professional resources for K-12 educators. Contact us for tailored, in-school training or to schedule an author for a workshop or conference. Visit www.maupinhouse.com for free lesson plan downloads.

🍎 Maupin House by

capstone·
professional

Maupin House Publishing, Inc. by Capstone Professional
1710 Roe Crest Drive
North Mankato, MN 56003

888-262-6135
www.maupinhouse.com
info@maupinhouse.com

Printed in the United States of America in Eau Claire, Wisconsin.
008376 072014

DEDICATION

This book is for "mijn geliefde zoon," Jesse, who is the inspiration for this story.
Remember third grade in "Nederland"? Even though you are now a grown man,
I still see that bright, courageous eight-year-old boy in you. "Ik hou van je."

and

For all you brave and wonderful souls who love to teach third grade.
You are the solid foundation blocks on which the rest of us build.

ACKNOWLEDGMENTS

First, I wish to thank my constant, loving editors—my husband, Chuck Kiester, and my mother, Perra Bell. Without your editing and "tersing," not to mention encouragement, I would not dare write. I love you both.

Second, I wish to thank the six teachers at Tommy Barfield Elementary School who teach in two multi-age, primary-program teams. They shared their expertise, ideas, and enthusiasm. Debbie Cooper, Jody McCarty, and Esther Scuderi taught one combined kindergarten/first-grade/second-grade class. Margo Barath, Diane Stone, and Barbara Stukey taught the second multi-age group. Thank you, ladies; you're super! Congratulations on the continued, high writing test scores at your school.

I especially with to thank Debbie Cooper who spoke to me at length about the magic she and her colleagues weave to teach students how to write correctly and confidently. Debbie also gave me some wonderful examples of her students' work and tested parts of this book with her class. I love visiting your classroom. Thank you for sharing your students with me.

A special thank you also goes to Diane Stone for her help with the example and Mayra Guadalupe Ortega Reyna, third-grader, who donated her work. Mayra enthusiastically shared with me her experiences with last December's Posada here in Florida. (She got to knock on the doors!) You made the "best corrections I ever saw." You did a wonderful job.

Next, I am indebted to "mi querida prima," Flo Ariessohn, for her invaluable help with the Spanish used in this story and also with the Mexican custom of Posada. I wish we weren't separated by an entire continent...

Je veux aussi remercier mon amie Sylvie Berli, Licenciée de l'Université de Genève, qui m'a aider à traduire des expressions espagñols en français.

And, a special thank you and hug goes to Emily Gorovsky, my super editor, who deftly helped me prune and organize this book. What a pleasure it is to work with you!

TABLE OF CONTENTS

IN THE BOOK

ON THE CD

An Introduction by Jane Bell Kiester

Ten Steps to Implement Caught'yas
in Your Classroom Explained

"Juan and Marie Join the Class," the entire,
uninterrupted Caught'ya story

Student Caught'yas

Student Assessment Chart

A Third-Grade Caught'ya Example

Twelve Writing Suggestions and Activities

*Grammar, Usage, and Mechanics Guide
(Everything You Never Wanted to Know about
Grammar, Usage, and Mechanics,
but I'm Going to Tell You Anyway)*

What You Will Find in This Book

The Caught'ya method teaches grammar, mechanics, usage, and vocabulary, all within the context of a story. Each Caught'ya, or story segment is one to four sentences long. Each segment has an error-laden "B" (for board) sentence with its corresponding, corrected "C" sentence that will serve as your teacher key. A list of skills is included above each Caught'ya for you to note what is being covered and what may need extra review. All vocabulary not on the Dolch Word List for third grade is listed before the Caught'yas so that you will know what words you may want to emphasize as they come up in your students' reading.

This **book** and the accompanying **CD** contain everything you need to use the Caught'ya method successfully with your third-grade students. In the book, you will find the following sections.

Caught'yas in a Nutshell briefly explains the Caught'ya method and lists ten easy steps for implementing the method in your class.

"Juan and Marie Join the Class," the entire, uninterrupted Caught'ya story, is printed so that you can familiarize yourself with the plot before you start the Caught'yas. Numbers displayed in the margin of the story correspond with the number of the Caught'ya for easy reference.

125 Student Caught'yas with Teacher's Key includes the board ("B") sentences and corrected ("C") sentences as well as a list of skills and bolded vocabulary for each Caught'ya.

On the **CD**, you'll find files that save you time, allow you to customize the Caught'yas to your needs, provide additional explanation, and present effective teaching ideas to supplement the daily Caught'yas.

An Introduction by Jane Bell Kiester shares the history of Caught'yas, why they're so successful, and how the method specifically works with third-graders.

Ten Steps to Implement Caught'yas in Your Classroom Explained will regale you with all the details and tricks necessary for implementing the Caught'ya method in your classroom.

"Juan and Marie Join the Class," the entire, uninterrupted Caught'ya story, is included so that you can print a copy to have in your classroom if you wish.

Student Caught'yas are provided so that you do not have to copy or type the Caught'yas and so that you easily can modify the sentences to fit your students' needs.

The **Student Assessment Chart** lets you track students' writing progress and note areas that need improvement.

A Third-Grade Caught'ya Example shows you what a student Caught'ya from Juan and Marie's story looks like.

Twelve Writing Suggestions and Activities help your students master the different types of prose in fun, effective, classroom-proven ways.

The *Grammar, Usage, and Mechanics Guide* (*Everything You Never Wanted to Know about Grammar, Usage, and Mechanics, but I'm Going to Tell You Anyway*) is a useful addendum I referred to almost daily when I taught Caught'yas (and I wrote it). The **GUM Guide** and the Caught'yas cover every skill listed in *Warriner's English Grammar and Composition: Complete Course*—the big white book that bored so many of us when we were in school. This also means that all the skills you are required by your state to teach (and then some) are covered. While in the third grade, you will not be teaching most of the skills listed and illustrated in this guide, you might find it useful for reference and teaching ideas. You can use it on the **CD** or print out a copy to put in your book.

Besides providing a quick reference for you, the **GUM Guide** contains simple examples you can use in your instruction and mnemonic devices to help your students learn some of the more difficult concepts.

Now I invite you to relax and read the rest of this book. I wish you and your students many giggles, a plethora of great vocabulary words, and much fluent writing.

Caught'yas in a Nutshell

A Quick Overview of the Caught'ya Method for Third Grade

The Caught'ya method teaches language skills in context in an integrated approach, making certain to cover all (and more) of your state's standards for third grade. Essentially, a Caught'ya is a sentence or two of an ongoing, funny story taught every day from a blackboard or overhead and copied and corrected by students in their editing journals.

In this book, there is a story that is specifically designed for third-grade when the social studies curriculum usually includes the study of cultures of other countries. In addition, many non-native English speakers who were in ESL classes for first and second grades often begin third grade in the regular classroom and can relate to this story about two children who must learn English as they did.

For each Caught'ya, there are the student sentences, the teacher's key, and a list of the skills being taught for that particular Caught'ya. Each sentence in the Caught'ya contains errors or omitted punctuation (like no period at the end of the sentence or a missing capital letter at the beginning). Each Caught'ya also includes several challenging words (those not on the Dolch Sight Word List for third grade). A few Caught'yas also contain simple literary devices such as similes.

The Caught'ya method is designed to allow *all* students to experience success and writing fluency. The teacher starts by reviewing the plot so far. You can use the uninterrupted story, **"Juan and Marie Join the Class,"** up to the Caught'ya you currently are teaching. Then the teacher introduces and elicits the meanings of the vocabulary word(s), reads the Caught'ya dramatically, reviews the need for a capital letter at the beginning of a sentence and a period at the end, goes over the types of sentences, and initiates a discussion of whether to begin a new paragraph in the story. You can change and modify the skills to fit the needs of your students (such as adding a literary device or leaving out punctuation).

As students copy and correct the Caught'ya in their editing journals, you walk around the room and give immediate, tinged-with-humor feedback (hugs included) to each student, providing quick mini-lessons, helping struggling students, and urging or challenging your more advanced students to find the errors on their own. This is the fun part!

Then, in their response journals, notebooks reserved especially for free-writing, students write about any topic they wish, but this is usually a topic suggested by the content of the Caught'ya.

Please note that, in the **Ten Steps to Implement Caught'yas in Your Classroom Explained** on the CD, editing and response journals will be explained in much more detail, including several ways to make the journals and establish their use in your classroom.

When nearly all of the students have completed the Caught'ya, written in their response journals, and received a comment from you, you return to the board or overhead. Together, you and students again discuss the meanings of the vocabulary words, acting them out if possible.

Then, with you presiding, the entire class reads the Caught'ya again several times and reviews missing punctuation and capitalization errors. Discuss as much as possible at this point, including the *reasons* and *rules* for each correction.

After the entire Caught'ya has been corrected communally, students can count the errors they missed the first time, i.e., when they attempted to correct the sentence on their own. Then they indicate the number of their initial errors in the margin of their papers. Several skills have been introduced, reinforced, or practiced; a new word or two has been learned; and maybe the class has enjoyed a giggle over the story, the vocabulary word, or the antics of the teacher as he or she cavorted around the room and checked each student's Caught'ya. And, after students have the routine of this entire procedure down pat, teachers find that their classes begin the day more smoothly with fewer discipline problems.

At the third-grade level, because of developmental maturity and because of having to copy the sentences, completing a Caught'ya takes about twenty to thirty minutes. For some students, especially the perfectionists and the underachievers, copying, correcting the Caught'ya in the editing journal, and then writing in the response journal takes a long time, but these activities are important to their development as writers. If you wish to reduce the time further or your students are taking too long to copy the Caught'ya, have your third-graders copy only one sentence of each two- to four-sentence Caught'ya, and do the rest orally with the class as a whole.

For continuity, you probably will want to do a Caught'ya every day as a routine exercise. This is a good idea, especially at the primary level, so that students do not forget the storyline. This also will make it easier to repeat skills *ad nauseam* until every student in the class masters them or begs for mercy.

Students soon get used to entering the classroom and immediately settling down to write the Caught'ya in their editing journals and compose a few paragraphs in their response journals. The Caught'ya routine shortens the "waste time" at the beginning of the day or after P.E., lunch, etc., when students are particularly rowdy. Because students crave the individual feedback their teacher gives while they are working on the Caught'ya sentences, they usually get to work very quickly.

Unfortunately, there are always a few students (usually the older ones) who get started quickly in order to "get it over with." With a little enthusiasm, you easily can discourage this attitude by making the Caught'ya a fun, laughter-filled activity. Young students tend to be more enthusiastic about the learning process, and honest older students have been known to confess in a weak moment that, even though they sometimes complain for the benefit of their peers, they really *do* enjoy doing the Caught'yas. Almost all students admit that they learn from them.

Sometimes students help each other with the errors in the Caught'ya. I liked to encourage this practice. You may hear whispered debates about whether and why a question mark is needed or hear a child reminding a friend to capitalize the first letter in a sentence, music to any teacher's ears.

EVALUATING THE CAUGHT'YAS

Evaluating the Caught'yas is as important as doing them. It is based on whether students catch the errors and mark them on their papers when the class reviews the sentences together, *not* on the number of errors made when students attempted to correct the Caught'ya on their own. In this way, no matter how weak their English skills are, students can experience success with this method. Your weakest students can excel if they listen and carefully correct their work. This is a wonderful inducement to pay attention.

There are several ways to evaluate Caught'yas in the third grade. They are explained in detail in **Step 9** of **Ten Steps to Implement Caught'yas in Your Classroom Explained** on the CD. You will want to collect the editing and response journals on a weekly basis, check them for errors, monitor students' writing fluency, and make positive comments in each child's journals. I suggest you keep a chart on each child's progress (see the sample **Student Assessment Chart** on the CD) that tracks the skills mastered, the number of more sophisticated vocabulary words used, and the increase in the number of sentences written. As you fill in the chart week after week, you will be delighted at the improvement in your students' writing ability.

TEN STEPS TO IMPLEMENT CAUGHT'YAS IN YOUR CLASSROOM

(For more detailed instructions, see **Ten Steps to Implement Caught'yas in Your Classroom Explained** on the CD.)

1. Read the complete Caught'ya story, "Juan and Marie Join the Class"; buy several story-related props for the classroom; and plan to do a Caught'ya every day from Juan and Marie's story.

2. Review the skills included in the Caught'yas, and decide which skills and vocabulary words you want to include; change the Caught'yas by using the CD; insert your students' names in the blanks provided; and begin.

3. Teach your students about editing and response journals, and make or buy one of each for every student. Prepare students for Juan and Marie's story.

4. Put the day's Caught'ya incorrectly ("B" sentence) on the board or overhead, and list beside it exactly what you want your students to do. Read the sentences dramatically; go over vocabulary words; and review paragraphing, capitalization, and end punctuation. Use kinesthetic techniques.

5. Students write the Caught'ya as correctly as they can in their editing journals. They then write in their response journals on any topic they want or one related to the Caught'ya.

6. Walk around the room, helping students with the Caught'ya, providing individual mini-lessons, commenting on each student's effort, giving hugs, and aiding with response journals.

7. Return to the board or overhead, and check the Caught'ya with the class, eliciting answers from students and again going over the vocabulary words. Use kinesthetic techniques.

8. Students correct all errors that they made, writing the corrections in a color other than the one initially used in the Caught'ya. They then count and indicate the number of errors in the margin of their editing journal page.

9. Collect the editing journals, make positive comments, and grade one Caught'ya. Note common errors your students make for later instruction.

10. Collect response journals, and write encouraging comments by at least one entry. Track each student's writing progress in their response journals using the Student Assessment Chart on the CD.

(85) Good work!
Watch those capital letters.   March 7 2005

Caught'ya Sentences #81-85

#81   Monday, March 7 2005
As he trudged to school with his heavy burden, Juan was happy. He couldn't wait to share his Mexican custom with his new friends.

#82   Tuesday, March 8, 2005
Happy because it was December, Juan happily anticipated the day at school and then going home that evening to celebrate Posada with his family, relatives, and Mexican neighbors.

#83   Wednesday, March 9, 2005
Suddenly the big fifth graders surrounded Juan. They wanted to know what was in the box that he lugged in his arms.   -10

#84   Thursday, March 10, 2005
panicked, croaked, and precious

ABSENT

#85   Friday, March 11, 2005
"Déjame solo. Basta!" Juan screeched out as he attempted to evade the bigger boys by running into the school.

"JUAN AND MARIE JOIN THE CLASS,"
THE ENTIRE, UNINTERRUPTED CAUGHT'YA STORY

Mexico
(pronounced "Mayhico")

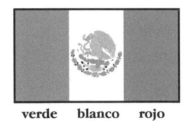

verde   blanco   rojo

La France
(pronounced "La Frahnce"–"n" is silent)

bleu   blanc   rouge

NOTE: The numbers in the margin correspond with the Caught'yas.

INTRO
As they approached the now-familiar buildings of _____ Elementary School, _____, _____, and _____ chattered merrily about the upcoming year. Their new teacher, _____, was popular. Many of their friends were going to be in their class, and it was a bright and sunny August morning. The three were soon joined by two others, _____ and _____, who continued the **animated conversation**. All five third-graders were eager to begin the new year.

"I sure hope _____ is as nice as my sister says," said _____.

"Yeah, she's (he's) supposed to be cool even when you have to work and such," said _____. "My brother says she laughs all the time and almost never yells unless you're *really, really* bad."

"Maybe we'll go on some neato field trips," added _____.

"And maybe my dog will fly," **retorted** _____.

Still chattering, the five friends approached the door of their new classroom. The teacher, _____, greeted them at the door with a big smile. She *looked* cool. Maybe they would like her as _____'s and _____'s sister and brother had said they would.

INTRO
"Welcome to the third grade," greeted the teacher. "You are the last five to arrive. Come on in and join the other students."

The five entered the classroom. Bright and cheerful posters hung from the walls. Fun-looking bulletin boards **advertised** subjects and skills. The alphabet in cursive **snaked** around the wall, high up near the ceiling. Even the windows **displayed** colorful signs. (*Teachers, add more description of your room. Use strong verbs like those above.*) The desks seemed a lot bigger than last year's desks. This was going to be an awesome year.

Right in the middle of the room, all the other kids **clustered** around something. What was it? _____ and _____ tried to get through the crush of kids, but _____ and _____ **blocked** their way. _____ tried to jump up to see what was in the middle of the circle of third-graders, but she couldn't jump high enough to see anything. What was in the middle of the crowd?

"OK," said their new teacher as she clapped her hands once for attention. "Let's sit down. Find your name on a desk and sit there. I have a surprise for you."

Suddenly, the tight circle of kids **dispersed**. Each student found a desk with his or her name on it and sat down. The bell rang, and all eyes turned to the place that had been the center of the circle of children. There, looking a little lost and afraid, were a boy and a girl—strangers. They looked like third-graders, but their clothes were kind of dorkish and definitely uncool. Who were they?

"Welcome to the third grade," _____, the teacher, repeated. "Some of you already have discovered the surprise, but let me introduce you to two new students at our school, Marie (*Teachers, gargle the "R"*) and Juan (*Huahn—"j" in Spanish is pronounced as an "h."*) not only are new to our school, they also are new to our country.

"Marie is from France, and Juan is from Mexico. France is in the continent called Europe, and Mexico is the country just to the south of the United States and touches our **borders**," the teacher continued. "Marie grew up speaking French, and Juan grew up speaking Spanish. Their English is not too good right now, but I know you can help them learn. That is why they are here. Try to understand that they don't understand much right now. Pretend it is you in a strange classroom in a strange country where you don't understand what is going on. Be kind. Be patient with them."

"Wow," said _____, "where is Juan's sombrero and sarape? Why isn't Marie dressed in a white apron and a tall hat like we saw in the pictures of France last year? Where is her beret? Why do they look like us, only like 'dorks' in uncool clothes?"

"Well," answered the teacher, "you will have to help teach Marie and Juan English first, and then you can ask them yourselves. I know that Juan is not wearing a sombrero and a sarape because people in Mexico only wear them to work outside in the hot sun or for holidays and festivals. They wear the same clothes that you do, but many of them wear uniforms to school.

"Uggg," said _____, "I hate uniforms."

"The aprons and hats were worn hundreds of years ago in France," she continued. "Now some people wear them on special days for special ceremonies only in certain parts of France. Some French men who live in the countryside still wear the berets, but women don't wear them. French people pronounce the name of their country 'Frahnce,' not 'France' as we say it. As for the 'dork' part, I'm sure you can introduce them to the styles third-grade students consider 'cool' to wear."

Marie raised her hand. "Madame," she asked. "Où est le WC?" (*Pronounced "Maah daahm, ooo eh le doobleh vay say?" Raise your voice at the end. It means, "Where is the*

Everyone in the class looked puzzled. What was Marie trying to ask? She obviously was talking to the teacher since she said, "Madame." But, what did the rest mean? Marie was looking more and more uncomfortable. She squirmed in her seat. She crossed her legs.

"La toilette (*pronounced "lah toahlet"*)," Marie added. _____ **blurted** out, "She has to go potty! 'Toilette' means 'toilet.' The words are almost the same!" He raised his hand to slap the hand of _____ to **celebrate** his smartness.

"I'll take her," said _____. "I can show her where it is. May _____ come too?"

As the three girls **traipsed** off to the bathroom, the rest of the class wondered what Marie and Juan would say next. Would they understand? Would they be able to help? They didn't know French or Spanish, so how were they going to teach the new students English? This was certainly going to be an interesting year! No one knew what would happen next. No one had any idea of the trouble not speaking English would cause…

The rest of the morning went **serenely**. _____, _____, and _____ helped Marie and Juan learn the names of their classmates. The morning passed **tranquilly**, that is, until Juan had to go to the restroom. He knew where the restrooms were **located**, and he raised his hand to be excused, just as he always did in his classroom in Mexico. When the teacher called his name, Juan asked, "Sala de baño," por favor?" He did not **comprehend** any English words except "yes" and "no." (*Sahlah day bahnyo, pour fahvor?*) Juan hoped his words were close enough to the English so that the teacher could **comprehend** what he was saying.

Since the words "sala de baño" in Spanish and "salle de bain" in French were **pronounced** a lot alike, Marie looked at Juan and smiled like a true friend. (*sahlah day bahnyo; sal duh bangh—make the "ngh" nasal*) Marie knew what Juan wanted, but she could not help him. She did not **comprehend** any English either.

Fortunately, _____, a fellow classmate, understood Juan and said in a loud voice, "Juan wants to go to the bathroom."

Luckily, Juan did not **comprehend** his **classmate** or he would have been embarrassed like a little boy.

The teacher, _____, **queried** Juan, "Do you know the way to the restroom, Juan?"

Juan did not understand her, but he heard his name, so he said, "Yes."

Like a **haughty hyena**, Juan, who spoke only Spanish, wanted to show off one of his two words of English to his new, American friends. The teacher pointed towards the **portal** of the classroom, and Juan got out of his desk and left the room.

Now, Juan knew where the restrooms were **located**. He did not know, however, which room was for the girls and which one was for the boys.

In Spanish the word for the restroom for the boys began with an "N" for "Niños." (*neenyos*) Here, the word on one of these doors started with a "B," and the word on the other door **commenced** with a "G."

Juan was **perplexed**. He did not know which door to enter. There were no (*or "weren't any"*) pictures under the words to help him. What could he do? He waited and waited to see if someone would come, **glancing** every once in a while down the hall toward his classroom like an **apprehensive aardvark**.

Why did Juan **linger** in front of the two doors? He waited to see which door a boy would enter and which door a girl would enter. No one came. Juan thought and thought, but he could not find any clue that would tell him which was the boys' **lavatory** and which was the girls' **lavatory**. Finally, Juan was **desperate** and **frantic**. He had to use the restroom so badly that he no longer cared which door was which.

Can you guess which door Juan entered? Yes, you are right. He went into the girls' **lavatory**.

Before Juan even stepped two **strides** into the room, some fifth-grade girls, who were close friends, opened the door of the bathroom. They **espied** Juan, and they stopped dead in their tracks.

The girls **shrieked** as one voice, "Ahhhhhhhhh, a boy!"

Juan, who was very **embarrassed**, **muttered**, "Lo siento mucho, muchachas," and he quickly exited the room. (**Low seeyento moocho, moochachaz**) He wanted to say, "Sorry, girls," in English, but he did not know the words.

"Who are you, you creep?" asked one of the older girls.

"Can't you read?" **queried** another in a voice that dripped with disgust.

"It's the girls' bathroom, you dummy," said the third girl.

Juan ran out to the hall and into the boys' **lavatory**. He could translate the word "stupid." It was close enough to the Spanish word "estupido." (**estoopeedoh**) He hid there, in the **odoriferous** boys' bathroom, until just before lunch when _____, _____, and _____ came in and took him back to the classroom.

While Juan **concealed** himself in the boys' **lavatory**, Marie **faced** some **dire dilemmas** of her own. Imagine what it would be like in a room full of kids, kids whom you could not **comprehend**! Imagine what it would be like not even to be able to read any signs, books, or posters on the walls! Would you be **apprehensive**?

Marie was **apprehensive**. _____, _____, _____, _____, and all the others looked like nice girls and boys. They smiled at her, but they asked Marie a lot of questions, questions Marie could not understand. Marie knew her **peers** were asking questions because their voices rose at the end of each sentence, but she couldn't **comprehend** what they asked.

Finally, she said in **exasperation**, "Quoi? Je ne vous comprends pas." In French this meant, "What? I do not understand you." (**"Kwoah? Juh nuh voo caw praw pah."** *Do not pronounce the "nt." It is a nasal sound in French.*)

"I think we've **perplexed** her," said _____.

"I don't know what Marie said, but she looks **apprehensive**," said _____.

"I agree," said _____.

"What can we do?" **queried** _____, who always was concerned about the feelings of others.

"Let's stop making **queries**," suggested _____.

"Yeah," **agreed** _____. "Why don't we teach her some words in English?"

Well, for the rest of the morning, instead of language arts, the class taught Marie a lot of English nouns. They taught her the following words: girl, boy, teacher, desk, **lectern**, blackboard, chalk, window, paper, pencil, book, and eraser.

In return, Marie taught her new class to sing the old, well-known song "Frère Jacques." (***Frayreh Jah-keh***) (Can you sing that **renowned** French song?) Marie taught her **peers** a few words in French, too. Of course, she taught them by pointing since she knew no English. In **camaraderie**, Marie taught her new friends the following words in French: le garçon (the boy) (***luh garsaunh—do not pronounce the "n" as it is nasal***), la fille (the girl) (***lah feeyuh***), le crayon (the pencil) (***luh crayaunh—do not pronounce the "n"***), and mon livre (my book) (***maunh leevruh—do not pronounce the "n"***).

_____, _____, and _____ had been sent to find Juan. Whey they all returned from the boys' lavatory just before lunch, the class stopped for a **brief respite** from the morning's work. They **devoured** lunch, went out to the playground, played on the **equipment**, visited with each other, and taught Juan and Marie outdoor words like "tree" and "sky."

It was a beautiful, sunny day, and Juan felt better to be out of the **putrescent** bathroom. A few fluffy clouds floated across the **azure** sky. Birds chirped **shrilly** as they flew overhead. Squirrels played and **cavorted** on the trunks and branches of oak trees that spread their wide arms towards the sky. Happy children's voices **chattered** all around Juan. Somewhere in the distance, a car horn tooted **faintly**, "Beep. Beep." It was a beautiful day, a day that would make anyone feel better. Juan breathed deeply and forgot his **embarrassment**.

Too soon, it was time to go inside, but Juan and Marie had made **firm** friends in their new, third-grade class.

The teacher, _____, blew a **shrill** whistle, "Tweeeet."

"It's time to go in," she said.

The whole class, including Juan and Marie, lined up at the door as quiet and **docile** as **dormice**.

The rest of the day passed **uneventfully**. Juan and Marie learned even more English, and they taught some French and Spanish to their **peers** in return. _____, _____, _____, and _____ pointed out more nouns like "pig," "dog," and "cat." They **inventively** used drawings in their reading books to **instruct** the foreign students. The teacher introduced a verb into their already **expanding** vocabulary—"to be." She taught Juan and Marie a few **adjectives**, too.

What is an **adjective**? Can you name a few of them? What adjectives do you think _____ taught Juan and Marie?

By the end of the day Juan and Marie could **utter** a few more things in English although they still knew fewer than fifty words in all, and they knew only one verb.

By the end of the week, the two **foreign** third-graders could say a few sentences. Now Juan could read the words on the **lavatory** doors!

The rest of the class also knew a few sentences in French and Spanish. They could **vocalize** "Tu es un cochon moche" in French and "Tu es uno cerdo feo" in Spanish. (***Too eh unh coshaunby mohsch and Too ess oono serdo fayoh***) Both meant, "You are an ugly pig." Now the third-graders could tease their friends and insult and **affront** their enemies.

Weeks went by. Marie and Juan learned more and more English from their teacher and from their **peers**. They could now speak in sentences. They still made **a plethora of** mistakes, though, when they spoke English.

Marie never could get the **prepositions** straight. She said that she "walked of home at school" instead of "walked from home to school" because "from" and "of" in French are **identical** words; so are "at" and "to." Because the French place most adjectives after the noun, Marie had a hard time with adjectives. She **persisted** in saying "a pig ugly" instead of "an ugly pig."

Juan, on the other hand, had a **predicament** with verbs. In Spanish there are two verbs for "is." Sometimes he said "I is ready" instead of "I am ready." He also had trouble with **pronunciation**.

Since everyone was included in the language lessons, everybody in _____'s third-grade class, including the teacher, learned a few **amusing** words and sentences in two **foreign** languages, French and Spanish. The **keen, intelligent** class learned to say "Yo soy superfino" in Spanish. They **attempted** to say "Je suis formidable" in French. (***Yo soy soupearfeeeno; Juh swee formidaaaabluh***) Those two **expressions** meant, "I am super," in their **respective** languages. The class also learned to say, "Tu es uncasse-pied" (***too eh cahss pee-ay***) in Marie's language. This meant, "You are a **severe** 'pain in the neck.'"

Juan taught the class to **declare**, "Eres una lata." (***Eyres oona lahtah—accent on first syllable in all words***)

The teacher, however, did not like this **expression** (even though it was in Spanish) because it had almost the same meaning as, "You are a pain in the rear." The class **whispered** and **murmured** it among themselves when they thought the teacher could not hear them. She could hear them, of course, because teachers always have **exemplary** hearing.

It was fun learning words in a foreign language. It was **challenging** to teach Juan and Marie English, but it also would **prove** to be dangerous! _____, _____, _____, and _____ **concluded** that so far, this *was*, indeed, the best year yet.

They did not know the **appalling** problems that were about to **ensue** between them and the fifth grade, all because of language problems.

It all began on the playground one **brisk** winter day. Juan was very excited. It was December, and he was going to share the Mexican tradition of Posada with his new American **cronies**. Posada began on December 16th and lasted until December 24th when there were lots of big parties. In a **mammoth** box almost as big as he was, Juan carried Mexican food for the whole class, a "piñata," and some "buñuelos." He had studied his English to be able to tell his classmates about the custom of Posada. (***piñata = peenyahtah—accent on "yah;" buñuelos = bunyouwailos—accent on "whale"***) Juan's uncle in Mexico had sent the "piñata" that was filled with "dulces" and little toys as well as a real "pan dulce." His mother had made **a plethora of** "buñuelos" and other **traditional** goodies for Juan's class just as mothers here bake cupcakes for birthday parties.

(*piñata = peenyatah; dulces = duelsayes; pan dulce = pahn duelsay; buñuelos = bunyouwailos—all accents on the second-to-last syllable*)

That winter morning, Juan **whistled** as he walked across the playground to the school building.

As he **trudged** to school with his heavy burden, Juan was happy. He couldn't wait to share his Mexican custom with his new friends. Finally, because it was December 16th, Juan happily **anticipated** the day at school and then going home that evening to celebrate Posada with his family, relatives, and Mexican neighbors.

Suddenly, big fifth-graders **surrounded** Juan. They wanted to know what was in the box that he **lugged** in his arms.

Juan **panicked**. He forgot all the English he had learned. His voice **croaked** in fear of losing all the **precious** things he had in his box.

"Déjame solo. Basta," he **squeaked** out as he **attempted** to **evade** the bigger boys by running into the school. (*Dayhamay so-low. Bahstah = Leave me alone. Enough.*)

Juan should have asked his father to walk him to school to **safeguard** the "golosinas." He should have spoken in English, but he did not. (*goloseenahs—accent on "see"*)

The bigger fifth-graders did not know that Juan was new in this country. They did not **discern** that he had spoken in Spanish. The fifth-grade, **rowdy bullies** thought that Juan had **insulted** them. They thought that he had called them "dookies" and a nasty word that **insulted** their mothers. This made the angry fifth-graders even more **irate**. They chased Juan all the way to his classroom.

"Well, what is this **fracas**?" asked Juan's teacher as she stood in the doorway to the room and grabbed Juan as he **sped** past her. "Are you **ruffians** picking on one of my third-graders?" she continued.

"No, Ma'am," said one of the fifth-graders.

"He **insulted** us," **blurted** out another of the bullies.

"I don't think Juan would do that **intentionally**," said the Juan's teacher. "Go to class, boys, and leave my students alone."

The biggest fifth-grader gave Juan a **dreadful stare** that said, "We're not finished with you, you little **critter**."

Juan was scared. His classmates were **apprehensive**, too. The big fifth-graders had **bullied** them before whenever a teacher was not around. Sometimes, some of the bigger children took the best goodies and all the cookies from third-graders' lunches, and they **consumed** them right in front of the **victims**.

"What can we do?" **whimpered** _____ to her friend _____ as the teacher closed the door of the classroom behind Juan.

"Those big kids really will come after us now," **whispered** _____ quietly so that the teacher could not hear.

The children became quiet as the teacher began class, but most of them were **agitated** by their fear of the bullies.

Except for a student occasionally looking **apprehensively** out the doorway, the rest of the day went very well in _____'s third-grade class.

Everyone enjoyed his or her treats, and the class heard all about the Mexican **tradition** of Posada. Juan explained that he was going to play the part of Joseph in the **procession**, and he even would wear a beard when he knocked on a neighbor's door that evening. Even after school nothing happened because the teacher walked everyone out. No third-graders were **threatened** that day, but they were still **wary**.

Juan decided that since this whole mess had been his fault, he wanted to fix the **predicament**. He had a plan. When Juan told his plan to his **peers**, Marie and the others offered to help put Juan's idea into action.

That night, Juan and Marie called their relatives in Mexico and in France and asked a big favor. Their **relatives** said, "Sí," and "Oui," both of which meant "Yes." (**See; Wee**)

The class explained the **ongoing dilemma** with the fifth-graders and asked the help of their teacher, _____.

She, too, said, "Yes."

For the next three weeks, _____'s third-grade class planned, prepared, **toiled**, and worked. Juan's mother ordered goodies from the local Mexican "panadería." (***pahnahdayreeyah—accent on the "ree"***) For those three weeks, the bullies **occasionally** snatched a cookie from a third-grader's lunch box or teased other students, but they always **glared** at Juan as if they wanted to beat him up. The larger bullies never could carry out their **implied threat**, however, because all the other third-graders hung around Juan all the time. Juan was never **unaccompanied** at school. There were always at least ten other third-grade students around him **whenever** he was out of the classroom.

Finally, everything was ready. The third grade **drafted** a letter to the fifth-grade students and sent it **via** their teacher who helped them write it.

_____ Elementary School
[*your school's address*]
[*your city*], [*your state*] [*your zip code*]

May ____, _____ (*put the correct date*)

The Fifth-grade Class
_____ Elementary School
[*your school's address*]
[*your city*], [*your state*] [*your zip code*]

Dear Fifth-Graders,

We apologize for the **misunderstanding** you had with Juan, one of our two new **foreign** students. We know that some of you have been mean to us in the past, but maybe it's because you like our cookies. We invite you to a party to let you meet Juan and Marie and to share some really yummy Mexican and French goodies with us.

Please come to our classroom Friday at two o'clock p.m. We want to get to know you, too. We also want to know what it is like to be a big fifth-grader.

Sincerely yours,

_____'s Third-grade Class

The next day, _____'s third-grade class received a reply to their **epistle**.

_____ Elementary School
[*your school's address*]
[*your city*], [*your state*] [*your zip code*]

May ____, _____ (*put the correct date*)

The Third-grade Class
_____ Elementary School
[*your school's address*]
[*your city*], [*your state*] [*your zip code*]

Dear Third-Graders,

We will **accept** your **invitation**. It's a nice, fun surprise for us. We'll come to your classroom Friday at two o'clock p.m. Did you say cookies?

_____'s Fifth-grade class
(the Cookie Monsters)

Friday finally arrived. Everyone in _____'s third-grade class came in early. Each student carried a **parcel**. All day long, instead of math, science, social studies, and language arts, the class practiced greetings in French and Spanish and prepared for the **awesome** party.

At two o'clock **precisely**, the fifth-graders and their teacher arrived at the door. Everything was ready for them.

As they opened the door of the classroom, Juan, Marie, and all the third-graders greeted their **guests** with cries of "Bienvenue" and "Hola." (***Beeahnvenoo—don't pronounce the first "n," stress the last syllable, and the "noo" rhymes with "moo"; Obla.***) Pictures, flags, and posters of France and Mexico **decorated** the room. Hundreds of Mexican and French **confections perched decoratively** on the desks. They had come from France and Mexico or had been made according to the recipes of Marie's and Juan's relatives. The room looked as if it had been **transported directly** from France and Mexico!

The fifth-graders were **astonished** and **delighted**. They ate the **confections**. The fifth-graders learned to sing songs in French and Spanish, and they **established** new **friendships** with the younger, smaller students. The fifth-graders apologized for their past **misdeeds** and promised never to **mistreat** third-graders again.

Now, the fourth-graders, who were a **mischievous** group, were another matter **entirely**...

125 Student Caught'yas with Teacher's Key

Caught'ya Vocabulary

Text to Be Read Aloud by the Teacher

animated	advertised	clustered	borders	traipsed
conversation	snaked	blocked	blurted	
retorted	displayed	dispersed	celebrate	

Caught'yas

1. serenely
2. tranquilly
3. located
4. comprehend
5. comprehend
6. pronounced
7. comprehend
8. fortunately
9. comprehend, embarrassed
10. queried
11. haughty, hyena
12. portal
13. located
14. commenced
15. perplexed
16. glancing, apprehensive, aardvark
17. linger
18. lavatory
19. desperate, frantic
20. lavatory
21. strides

22. espied, shrieked
23. embarrassed, muttered
24. queried, disgust
25. lavatory
26. odoriferous
27. concealed, lavatory, faced, dire, dilemmas
28. comprehend
29. apprehensive
30. apprehensive, comprehend
31. peers
32. exasperation
33. perplexed, apprehensive
34. queried
35. queries, agreed
36. lectern
37. renowned
38. peers
39. camaraderie
40. brief, respite
41. devoured, equipment

42. putrescent
43. azure, shrilly
44. cavorted
45. chattered, faintly
46. embarrassment
47. firm
48. shrill
49. docile, dormice
50. uneventfully, peers
51. inventively, instruct
52. expanding, adjectives
53. adjective
54. utter
55. foreign, lavatory
56. vocalize
57. affront
58. peers
59. a plethora of
60. prepositions
61. identical
62. persisted
63. predicament
64. pronunciation
65. amusing, foreign
66. keen, intelligent, attempted
67. expressions, respective
68. severe
69. declare
70. expression
71. whispered, murmured
72. exemplary
73. challenging, prove
74. concluded
75. appalling, ensue
76. brisk
77. cronies
78. mammoth
79. a plethora of, traditional
80. whistled
81. trudged
82. anticipated
83. surrounded, lugged
84. panicked, croaked, precious

85. squeaked, attempted, evade
86. safeguard
87. discern
88. rowdy, bullies, insulted
89. irate
90. fracas, sped
91. ruffians
92. insulted, blurted
93. intentionally
94. dreadful, stare, critter
95. apprehensive
96. bullied
97. consumed, victims
98. whimpered
99. whispered
100. agitated
101. apprehensively
102. tradition, procession
103. threatened, wary
104. predicament
105. peers
106. relatives
107. ongoing, dilemma
108. toiled
109. occasionally, glared
110. implied, threat
111. unaccompanied, whenever
112. drafted, via
113. misunderstanding, foreign
114. epistle
115. accept, invitation
116. parcel
117. awesome
118. precisely
119. guests
120. decorated, confections, perched, decoratively
121. transported, directly
122. astonished, delighted, confections
123. established, friendships
124. misdeeds, mistreat
125. mischievous, entirely

This text is to be read to the class by the teacher at the beginning of the year to introduce the background of the story. Vocabulary that is beyond a third-grade level has been bolded the first time each challenging word appears. Since this part of the story is intended to be read orally by an adult, these words are pointed out only to highlight their level of difficulty. You might want to change the idioms to the ones your current students use. I think "dork," for example, is already outdated. Insert the names of your students in the blanks to personalize the story.

> **NOTE #1:** *"Rouge" (pronounced like the rouge you put on your cheeks) and "rojo" (roho) = red; blanc (blahunh—"n" and "c" are silent) and "blanco" (blahnco) = white; and "bleu" (blooh) and "azul" (azool) = blue.*
>
> **NOTE #2:** *"Juan" is pronounced "Huahn," and Marie is pronounced "Mahree" with a gargled "R."*

"JUAN AND MARIE JOIN THE CLASS"

As they approached the now-familiar buildings of _____ Elementary School, _____, _____, and _____ chattered merrily about the upcoming year. Their new teacher, _____, was popular. Many of their friends were going to be in their class, and it was a bright and sunny August morning. The three were soon joined by two others, _____ and _____, who continued the **animated conversation**. All five third-graders were eager to begin the new year.

"I sure hope _____ is as nice as my sister says," said _____.

"Yeah, she's (*he's*) supposed to be cool even when you have to work and such," said _____. "My brother says she laughs all the time and almost never yells unless you're *really, really* bad."

"Maybe we'll go on some neato field trips," added _____.

"And maybe my dog will fly," **retorted** _____.

Still chattering, the five friends approached the door of their new classroom. The teacher, _____, greeted them at the door with a big smile. She *looked* cool. Maybe they would like her as _____'s and _____'s sister and brother had said they would.

"Welcome to the third grade," greeted the teacher. "You are the last five to arrive. Come on in and join the other students."

The five entered the classroom. Bright and cheerful posters hung from the walls. Fun-looking bulletin boards **advertised** subjects and skills. The alphabet in cursive **snaked** around the wall, high up near the ceiling. Even the windows **displayed** colorful signs. (***Teachers, add more description of your room. Use strong verbs like those above.***) The desks seemed a lot bigger than last year's desks. This was going to be an awesome year.

Right in the middle of the room, all the other kids **clustered** around something. What was it? _____ and _____ tried to get through the crush of kids, but _____ and _____ **blocked** their way. _____ tried to jump up to see what was in the middle of the circle of third-graders, but she couldn't jump high enough to see anything. What was in the middle of the crowd?

"OK," said their new teacher as she clapped her hands once for attention. "Let's sit down. Find your name on a desk and sit there. I have a surprise for you."

Suddenly, the tight circle of kids **dispersed**. Each student found a desk with his or her name on it and sat down. The bell rang, and all eyes turned to the place that had been the center of the circle of children. There, looking a little lost and afraid, were a boy and a girl—strangers. They looked like third-graders, but their clothes were kind of dorkish and definitely uncool. Who were they?

"Welcome to the third grade," _____, the teacher, repeated. "Some of you already have discovered the surprise, but let me introduce you to two new students at our school, Marie (***Teachers, gargle the "R"***) and Juan (***Huahn—"j" in Spanish is pronounced as an "h."***) not only are new to our school, they also are new to our country.

"Marie is from France, and Juan is from Mexico. France is in the continent called Europe, and Mexico is the country just to the south of the United States and touches our **borders**," the teacher continued. "Marie grew up speaking French, and Juan grew up speaking Spanish. Their English is not too good right now, but I know you can help them learn. That is why they are here. Try to understand that they don't understand much right now. Pretend it is you in a strange classroom in a strange country where you don't understand what is going on. Be kind. Be patient with them."

"Wow," said _____, "where is Juan's sombrero and sarape? Why isn't Marie dressed in a white apron and a tall hat like we saw in the pictures of France last year? Where is her beret? Why do they look like us, only like 'dorks' in uncool clothes?"

"Well," answered the teacher, "you will have to help teach Marie and Juan English first, and then you can ask them yourselves. I know that Juan is not wearing a sombrero and a sarape because people in Mexico only wear them to work outside in the hot sun or for holidays and festivals. They wear the same clothes that you do, but many of them wear uniforms to school.

"Uggg," said _____, "I hate uniforms."

"The aprons and hats were worn hundreds of years ago in France," she continued. "Now some people wear them on special days for special ceremonies only in certain parts of France. Some French men who live in the countryside still wear the berets, but women don't wear them. French people pronounce the name of their country 'Frahnce,' not 'France' as we say it. As for the 'dork' part, I'm sure you can introduce them to the styles third-grade students consider 'cool' to wear."

Marie raised her hand. "Madame," she asked. "Où est le WC?" (***Pronounced "Maah daahm, ooo eh le doobleh vay say?" Raise your voice at the end. It means, "Where is the WC, or bathroom?" WC stands for "water closet," which the toilet was originally called in Europe.***)

Everyone in the class looked puzzled. What was Marie trying to ask? She obviously was talking to the teacher since she said, "Madame." But, what did the rest mean? Marie was looking more and more uncomfortable. She squirmed in her seat. She crossed her legs.

"La toilette (***pronounced "lah toahlet"***)," Marie added. _____ **blurted** out, "She has to go potty! 'Toilette' means 'toilet.' The words are almost the same!" He raised his hand to slap the hand of _____ to **celebrate** his smartness.

"I'll take her," said _____. "I can show her where it is. May _____ come too?"

As the three girls **traipsed** off to the bathroom, the rest of the class wondered what Marie and Juan would say next. Would they understand? Would they be able to help? They didn't know French or Spanish, so how were they going to teach the new students English? This was certainly going to be an interesting year! No one knew what would happen next. No one had any idea of the trouble not speaking English would cause…

Stop reading out loud here.

125 Caught'yas for Third Grade

Some last-minute reminders

→ Since all the sentences need capital letters at the beginning and some sort of punctuation at the end, these skills are *not* repeated in the list of skills to the left of each Caught'ya. Similarly, capitalization of proper nouns and the pronoun "I" also are not listed.

→ You need to go over the above four skills *every* day without fail, even after *all* your students consistently put capital letters where they belong and always use end punctuation. Ask your weakest students to identify these points when you go over the Caught'ya with the class. They will be thrilled to supply information they know. These skills cannot be taught enough.

→ The phonetic pronunciations for the French and Spanish words are given in the corrected sentence in bold, italicized type. They are for your eyes only so that you can pronounce the words correctly and teach them to your students. Third grade is the perfect time to begin learning other languages.

→ In the notes above each Caught'ya, I have indicated the types of sentences in that Caught'ya. Go over this skill daily. Ask your students to produce their own example of whatever type of sentence is included in the day's Caught'ya. You might even want to target varying sentence types in your students' writing.

B = Sentence for the board   **C = Corrected version of the Caught'ya**

---

1. serenely

Paragraph – beginning of story, time change

Types of sentences – simple; simple (compound subject)

Commas – noun series

Verb tense – add "ed" to end of regular verbs to put in past tense; "went" is past tense of verb "to go"

Spelling rules – "i" before "e" except after "c," and "**neighbor**," "**weigh**," and "**their**" are "weird"; form most plurals by adding "s"; homophones (their/there/they're)

Other skills – strong verb practice; teach homophones "their/there/they're"

B – the rest of the morning went **serenely**. _____, _____ and _____ helped marie and juan learn the names of their classmates

C – The rest of the morning went **serenely**. _____, _____, and _____ helped Marie and Juan learn the names of their classmates.

2. tranquilly

NO PARAGRAPH – same person speaking (narrator), same topic

TYPE OF SENTENCE – complex (subordinate clause at the end)

COMMAS – interrupter

VERB TENSE – add "ed" to end of regular verbs to put in past tense; "had" is past tense of irregular verb "to have"

SPELLING RULE – "until" has one "l"

OTHER SKILL – difference between "past" and "passed"

B – the morning passed **tranquilly** that is until juan had to go to the restroom.

C – The morning passed **tranquilly**, that is, until Juan had to go to the restroom.

---

3. located

NO PARAGRAPH – same person speaking (narrator), same topic

TYPE OF SENTENCE – compound

COMMAS – compound sentence; extra info

VERB TENSE – add "ed" to end of regular verbs to put in past tense; "did" is past tense of irregular verb "to do"; "were" is past tense of verb "to be"; "knew" is past tense of verb "to know"

SPELLING RULES – compound words (restroom, classroom); homophones (new/knew/gnu)

OTHER SKILLS – go over compound words (restroom, classroom); coordinating conjunctions (see note after Caught'ya #9)

B – he knew where the restrooms were **located** and he raised his hand to be excused just as he always did in his classroom in mexico

C – He knew where the restrooms were **located**, and he raised his hand to be excused, just as he always did in his classroom in Mexico.

---

4. comprehend

NO PARAGRAPH – same person speaking, same subject

TYPES OF SENTENCES – complex (subordinate clause at beginning); simple

PUNCTUATION – use of quotation marks around what is said out loud; use quotation marks around isolated words that are referred to

CAPITALIZATION – always capitalize the first letter of a quote unless it is a continuation; always capitalize the names of languages

COMMAS – appositive; subordinate clause at beginning (long introductory adverb); quote

VERB TENSE – add "ed" to end of regular verbs to put in past tense; "said" is past tense of irregular verb "to say"

SPELLING RULES – difference between accept/except; most plurals formed with "s"

OTHER SKILLS – strong verb practice; negatives; periods and commas always go inside quotation marks; words out of context of a sentence must be put in quotes; abbreviations of titles (Mr., Ms., Miss, Mrs. before teacher's name)

B – when the teacher called his name juan asked sala de baño por favor? he did not **comprehend** any english words except "yes" and "no"

C – When the teacher called his name, Juan asked, "Sala de baño," por favor?" He did not **comprehend** any English words except "yes" and "no." (*Sahlah day bahnyo, pour fahvor?*)

5. comprehend

NO PARAGRAPH – same subject

TYPE OF SENTENCE – complex (subordinate clause at the end = no comma)

CAPITALIZATION – always capitalize the names of languages

VERB TENSE – add "ed" to end of regular verbs to put in past tense; "was" is past tense of irregular verb "to be"

SPELLING RULE – difference between "hoped" and "hopped"

B – Juan hoped that his words were close enough to the english so that the teacher could **comprehend** what he was saying

C – Juan hoped his words were close enough to the English so that the teacher could **comprehend** what he was saying.

---

6. pronounced

PARAGRAPH – new subject

TYPE OF SENTENCE – complex (subordinate clause at beginning = comma) with compound verb

CAPITALIZATION – always capitalize the names of languages

COMMAS – subordinate clause at beginning (long introductory adverb)

VERB TENSE – add "ed" to end of regular verbs to put in past tense; "was" is past tense of irregular verb "to be"

SPELLING RULES – "a lot" is 2 words; "i" before "e" except after "c," and "**nei**ghbor," "w**ei**gh," and "th**ei**r" are "w**ei**rd"

LITERARY DEVICE – simile

B – since the words "sala de baño" in spanish and "salle de bain" in french were **pronounced** alot alike marie looked at juan and smiled like a true freind

C –   Since the words "sala de baño" in Spanish and "salle de bain" in French were **pronounced** a lot alike, Marie looked at Juan and smiled like a true friend. (***sahlah day bahnyo; sal duh bangh— make the "ngh" nasal***)

---

7. comprehend

NO PARAGRAPH – same subject

TYPES OF SENTENCES – compound; simple

CAPITALIZATION – always capitalize the names of languages

COMMAS – compound sentence

VERB TENSE – add "ed" to end of regular verbs to put in past tense; "knew" is past tense of verb "to know"

SPELLING RULES – homophones (new/knew/gnu)

OTHER SKILLS – strong verb practice; negatives; subject vs. object pronouns (she/her and he/him); coordinating conjunctions (for, and, nor, but, or, yet, so—see note after Caught'ya #9)

B – marie knew what juan wanted but she could not help him. she did not **comprehend** any english either

C – Marie knew what Juan wanted, but she could not help him. She did not **comprehend** any English either.

8. fortunately

PARAGRAPH – new subject

TYPE OF SENTENCE – simple (compound verb)

CAPITALIZATION – first letter in quote

PUNCTUATION – use of quotation marks around what is said out loud

COMMAS – introductory adverb (optional); appositive; quote

VERB TENSE – "understood" is past tense of irregular verb "to understand"; "said" is past tense of verb "to say"; switch to present tense for quote

SPELLING RULE – compound words

OTHER SKILL – punctuation of quotes

B – **fortunately** _____ a fellow classmate understood juan and said in a loud voice juan wants to go to the bathroom

C – **Fortunately,** _____, a fellow classmate, understood Juan and said in a loud voice, "Juan wants to go to the bathroom."

---

9. comprehend, embarrassed

PARAGRAPH – new person speaking (narrator)

TYPE OF SENTENCE – compound

COMMAS – introductory adverb (optional); compound sentence

VERB TENSE – add "ed" to end of regular verbs to put in past tense; correct use of conditional tense to indicate possible situation

OTHER SKILLS – begin teaching coordinating conjunctions; compound word

LITERARY DEVICE – simile

B – luckily juan did not **comprehend** his classmate or he would have been **embarrassed** like a little boy

C – Luckily, Juan did not **comprehend** his classmate or he would have been **embarrassed** like a little boy.

> **NOTE:** *It is a good idea to teach very young students the seven coordinating conjunctions used to make compound sentences. You can recall them using the mnemonic device "FANBOYS" (for, and, nor, but, or, yet, so). Once learned, students can be taught to put commas before them only if they are in a series or there is a compound sentence, to recognize a compound sentence, not to capitalize them in a title, and never, never to begin a sentence with one. I tell my students that they can do two things at age sixteen: drive, and begin an occasional sentence with a coordinating conjunction. Chant these conjunctions over and over again with your students. Memorization gives young students (and those of any age) ownership of a skill. I suggest your students learn them and then chant them every time one appears in a Caught'ya. The teachers who follow you will want to kiss your toes in gratitude!*

10. queried

2 PARAGRAPHS – new subject and persons speaking

TYPES OF SENTENCES – simple question (quote); compound

CAPITALIZATION – first letter in quote

PUNCTUATION – use of quotation marks around what is said out loud

COMMAS – appositive; quote; direct address; compound sentence; compound sentence; quote

VERB TENSE – add "ed" to end of regular verbs to put in past tense; "heard" is past tense of irregular verb "to hear"; switch to present tense for quote

SPELLING RULES – compound words; homophones (know/no)

OTHER SKILLS – strong verb practice; silent "e" making previous vowel long in "queried"; review coordinating conjunctions; note punctuation marks inside quotation marks; abbreviations of titles (Mr., Ms., Miss, Mrs. before the teacher's name)

B – the teacher _____ **queried** juan. do you know the way to the restroom juan. juan did not understand her but he heard his name so he said yes

C – The teacher, _____, **queried** Juan, "Do you know the way to the restroom, Juan?" Juan did not understand her, but he heard his name, so he said, "Yes."

---

11. haughty, hyena

PARAGRAPH – new person speaking (narrator)

TYPE OF SENTENCE – simple

CAPITALIZATION – always capitalize names of languages and countries/nationalities

COMMAS – introductory phrase; adjective clause with relative pronoun (who); 2 adjectives not separated by "and" where the second is not color, age, or linked to the noun

VERB TENSE – add "ed" to end of regular verbs to put in past tense; "spoke" is past tense of irregular verb "to speak"

SPELLING RULES – homophones (two/to/too and new/knew/gnu); most words form plural by adding "s"; "i" before "e" except after "c," and "neighbor," "weigh," and "their" are "weird"

OTHER SKILLS – do not begin a sentence with a coordinating conjunction (FANBOYS); possessive pronouns (his); "who" is used as the subject of a verb and "whom" is used as the object of a verb ("that" is used as subject or object but not to refer to people); write out numbers up to 121

LITERARY DEVICES – simile; alliteration

B – and like a **haughty hyena** juan who spoke only spanish wanted to show off one of his 2 words of english to his new american friends

C – Like a **haughty hyena**, Juan, who spoke only Spanish, wanted to show off one of his two words of English to his new, American friends.

12. portal

No PARAGRAPH – same speaker and topic

TYPE OF SENTENCE – compound (with compound verb in 2nd half)

COMMAS – compound sentence

VERB TENSE – add "ed" to end of regular verbs to put in past tense; "got" is past tense of irregular verb "to get"; "left" is past tense of verb "to leave"

SPELLING RULE – compound word

OTHER SKILLS – do not begin a sentence with a coordinating conjunction (FANBOYS); review coordinating conjunctions; strong verb practice; towards vs. toward (interchangeable); possessive pronouns (his)

B – so the teacher pointed towards the **portal** of the classroom and juan got out of his desk and left the room

C – The teacher pointed towards the **portal** of the classroom, and Juan got out of his desk and left the room.

---

13. located

PARAGRAPH – new topic

TYPES OF SENTENCES – simple; simple

COMMAS – introductory adverb used as interjection; interrupter (however)

VERB TENSE – "was" is past tense of irregular verb "to be"; "knew" is past tense of verb "to know"

SPELLING RULES – homophones (new/knew/gnu and know/no); most words form plurals by adding "s"; compound words

OTHER SKILL – subject/verb agreement ("which one *was*" since "one" is singular)

B – now juan knew where the restrooms were **located**. he did not know however which room was for the girls and which one were for the boys

C – Now, Juan knew where the restrooms were **located**. He did not know, however, which room was for the girls and which one was for the boys.

NOTE #1: *Students use the conditional tense as a substitute for the past ("When I was younger, I would play with my brother"). This is wrong. You either played (past tense) with your brother or not. "Would play" means that it has not happened yet. Please stop this practice early in your students' writing.*

NOTE #2: *At the third-grade level, students are not yet ready to learn the difference between "who" and "whom." Thus, I have always written them correctly in the "B" sentences. Students can, however, learn that you never use "that" to refer to a person even though they hear people use it all the time.*

---

14. commenced

PARAGRAPH – narrator aside

TYPES OF SENTENCES – simple; compound

CAPITALIZATION – single letters are always capitalized; languages

PUNCTUATION – use of quotation marks around single letters and words out of context; note commas and periods always go inside quotation marks

COMMAS – introductory adverb; compound sentence

VERB TENSE – add "ed" to end of regular verbs to FANBOYS); point out need for "an" with single letter "N"; use of demonstrative pronouns "this," "that," "these," "those"

LITERARY DEVICE – use of synonyms ("portal" and "door," "started" and "commenced")

B – in spanish the word for the restroom for the boys began with an n for niños. hear the word on one of these doors started with a b and the word on the other door **commenced** with a g

C – In Spanish the word for the restroom for the boys began with an "N" for "Niños." Here, the word on one of these doors started with a "B," and the word on the other door **commenced** with a "G." (*neenyos*)

---

15. perplexed

PARAGRAPH – back to Juan

TYPES OF SENTENCES – simple; simple; simple; simple question

PUNCTUATION – question mark needed in question

VERB TENSE – "was" is past tense of irregular verb "to be"; "did" is past tense of verb "to do"

SPELLING RULES – homophones (there/their/they're and know/no); teach the spelling of "there/their/they're"

OTHER SKILL – use of negative (never use a double negative)

B – juan was **perplexed**. he did not know which door to enter. there werent no pictures under the words to help him. what could he do

C – Juan was **perplexed**. He did not know which door to enter. There were no (or "weren't any") pictures under the words to help him. What could he do?

NOTE: *Teaching the dreaded "there/their/they're" to students requires much repetition and ingenuity. My students never knew when I misspelled them (and other common homophones) in the Caught'yas. They got almost indignant when I occasionally spelled them correctly! I liked to tell students that "their" has the little word "heir" in it. We looked up that word. It means that someone will own something. "Their" is possessive. It means that "they" own something. "There" has the little word "here" in it. I stressed to students that if they could substitute "here" for "there" in a sentence, then they were using the correct form. As for "they're," I simply insisted that the apostrophe stands for an "a." If students put in the "a," it reads "they are" which is the correct definition of the word. Be inventive. I'm sure you can think of other ways to teach these difficult-to-understand homophones.*

16. glancing, apprehensive, aardvark

No PARAGRAPH – same topic
TYPES OF SENTENCES – simple (compound verb)
COMMAS – participial phrase
VERB TENSE – add "ed" to end of regular verbs to put in past tense
SPELLING RULE – compound word
PRONOUNS – go over possessive pronouns (his)
OTHER SKILLS – use the article "an" before a noun that begins with a vowel; introduce the idea of prepositions and prepositional phrases
LITERARY DEVICES – simile; alliteration

B – he waited and waited to see if someone would come **glancing** every once in a while down the hall toward his classroom like a **apprehensive aardvark**

C – He waited and waited to see if someone would come, **glancing** every once in a while down the hall toward his classroom like an **apprehensive aardvark**.

---

17. linger

PARAGRAPH – narrator aside
TYPES OF SENTENCES – simple (question); simple with compound objects
PUNCTUATION – need for a question mark in a question
VERB TENSE – add "ed" to end of regular verbs to put in past tense; use of conditional tense to denote possible future action (would)
OTHER SKILL – homophones (to/two/too; see/sea; which/witch)
LITERARY DEVICE – questioning to involve reader in story

B – why did juan **linger** in front of the two doors. he waited to see which door a boy would enter and which door a girl would enter

C – Why did Juan **linger** in front of the two doors? He waited to see which door a boy would enter and which door a girl would enter.

---

18. lavatory

No PARAGRAPH – same topic
TYPES OF SENTENCES – simple; compound with compound object
COMMAS – compound sentence
VERB TENSE – irregular past tense of verb "to think"
PLURAL VS. POSSESSIVE – go over rules for possessive of plural nouns
OTHER SKILLS – never begin a sentence with a conjunction (but) as they are meant to join; "no one" is two words; review FANBOYS

B – but no one came. juan thought and thought but he could not find any clue that would tell him which was the boys **lavatory** and which was the girls **lavatory**

C – No one came. Juan thought and thought, but he could not find any clue that would tell him which was the boys' **lavatory** and which was the girls' **lavatory**.

19. desperate, frantic

NO PARAGRAPH – same topic, narrator still speaking

TYPES OF SENTENCES – simple; complex

COMMAS – introductory adverb; none needed after "badly" (subordinate clause "that he no..." at end)

VERB TENSE – "was" is past tense of irregular verb "to be"; "had" is past tense of verb "to have"; note use of infinitive (to use)

SPELLING RULES – compound word (restroom); homophones (which/witch)

OTHER SKILLS – adverb vs. adjective (badly/bad); go over adverbs (finally, badly)

B – finally juan was **desperate** and **frantic**. he had to use the restroom so bad that he no longer cared which door was which

C – Finally, Juan was **desperate** and **frantic**. He had to use the restroom so badly that he no longer cared which door was which.

20. lavatory

PARAGRAPH – narrator aside questioning the reader

TYPES OF SENTENCES – simple; simple; simple

PUNCTUATION – need for question mark at end of question

COMMAS – introductory word "yes"

VERB TENSE – add "ed" to end of regular verbs to put in past tense; switch to present tense for narrator aside then back to past for continuation of story; "went" is the past tense of the verb "to go"

SPELLING RULE – homophones (right/rite/write)

OTHER SKILLS – possessive of plural noun; wrong

VERB TENSE – (story in past)

LITERARY DEVICE – narrator aside/question to involve reader in story

B – can you guess which door juan entered. yes you are right. he goes into the girls **lavatory**

C –   Can you guess which door Juan entered? Yes, you are right. He went into the girls' **lavatory**.

21. strides

PARAGRAPH – new person speaking (no longer narrator aside)

TYPE OF SENTENCE – complex (subordinate clause at beginning)

COMMAS – subordinate clause at beginning of sentence; adjective clause with relative pronoun "who" (extra information about noun "girls")

VERB TENSE – add "ed" to end of regular verbs to put in past tense; "was" is past tense of irregular verb "to be"; switch to present tense for quote

SPELLING RULES – consonant/vowel/consonant = double 2nd consonant when suffix is added; "i" before "e" except after "c," and "**neighbor**," "**weigh**," and "**their**" are "**weird**"; compound word; add "s" to make most plurals (girls, friends)

OTHER SKILLS – write out numbers to 121; strong verb practice; note hyphen in two words acting as one

B – before juan even stepped 2 **strides** into the room some fifth-grade girls who were close freinds opened the door of the bathroom

C –   Before Juan even stepped two **strides** into the room, some fifth-grade girls, who were close friends, opened the door of the bathroom.

22. espied, shrieked

NO PARAGRAPH – same topic; PARAGRAPH – new persons speaking

TYPES OF SENTENCES – compound; simple quote

CAPITALIZATION – always capitalize the beginning of a quote

PUNCTUATION – use of quotation marks around what is said out loud; need for exclamation mark after obvious shout

COMMAS – compound sentence; before quote; after interjection

VERB TENSE – add "ed" to end of regular verbs to put in past tense

SPELLING RULES – consonant/vowel/consonant = double 2nd consonant when suffix is added; most nouns form plural by adding "s"; homophones (their/there/they're)

OTHER SKILLS – strong verb practice; note deliberate use of fragment in quote; review FANBOYS

LITERARY DEVICE – onomatopoeia (putting a sound into words)

B – they **espied** juan and they stopped dead in their tracks. the girls **shrieked** as one voice ahhhhhhhhh a boy

C – They **espied** Juan, and they stopped dead in their tracks.
The girls **shrieked** as one voice, "Ahhhhhhhhh, a boy!"

23. embarrassed, muttered

PARAGRAPH – new person speaking

TYPES OF SENTENCES – compound; compound

CAPITALIZATION – capitalize at beginning of quote; always capitalize the name of a language

PUNCTUATION – use of quotation marks around what is said out loud

COMMAS – adjective clause with relative pronoun "who" (extra information about a noun;) direct address ("muchachas"); compound sentence; before quote; direct address ("girls"); compound sentence

VERB TENSE – add "ed" to end of regular verbs to put in past tense; "did" is past tense of verb "to do"

SPELLING RULE – hard-to-spell word "embarrassed"

OTHER SKILLS – strong verb practice; review FANBOYS

B – juan who was very **embarrassed muttered** lo siento mucho, muchachas and he quickly exited the room. he wanted to say sorry girls in english but he did not know the words

C –   Juan, who was very **embarrassed**, **muttered**, "Lo siento mucho, muchachas," and he quickly exited the room. He wanted to say, "Sorry, girls," in English, but he did not know the words. (***Low seeyento moocho, moochachaz***)

24. queried, disgust

3 PARAGRAPHS – 3 persons speaking

TYPES OF SENTENCES – all simple quotations

CAPITALIZATION – always capitalize first letter of a quote

PUNCTUATION – use of quotation marks around what is said out loud; question marks needed at the end of question

COMMAS – direct address; direct address; quote

VERB TENSE – add "ed" to end of regular verbs to put in past tense; "said" is past tense of verb "to say"; switch to present tense for quote

SPELLING RULES – homophones (it's/its); consonant/vowel/consonant = double 2nd consonant when suffix added (dripped); compound word

CONTRACTION – "can't" means "cannot"; "it's" means "it is"

PLURAL VS. POSSESSIVE – plural possessive (girls)—teach that possessives always have to have something to possess

OTHER SKILLS – comparatives (old/older/oldest); possessive of plural noun; teach ordinal numbers (first, second, third, etc.)

LITERARY DEVICE – alliteration (d, d); anadiplosis (repeating a word or phrase for emphasis)

B – who are you you creep. asked one of the older girls. cant you read **queried** another in a voice that dripped with **disgust**. its the girls bathroom you dummy said the third girl

C – "Who are you, you creep?" asked one of the older girls.
"Can't you read?" **queried** another in a voice that dripped with **disgust**.
"It's the girls' bathroom, you dummy," said the third girl.

---

25. lavatory

PARAGRAPH – narrator speaking instead of girl

TYPES OF SENTENCES – simple (compound object); simple; simple

CAPITALIZATION – always capitalize the names of countries and nationalities

PUNCTUATION – use of quotation marks around word out of context of sentence; periods and commas always go inside quotes, even in one-word quotes

COMMAS – no comma before "and" unless a compound sentence or a list

VERB TENSE – "ran" is past tense of verb "to run"; "could" is past tense of verb "can"; "was" is past tense of irregular verb "to be"

PLURAL VS. POSSESSIVE – "boys'" is plural possessive, not to be confused with the plural "boys" since the lavatory is "owned" (possessed) by the boys

B – juan ran out to the hall and into the boys **lavatory**. he could translate the word "stupid." it was close enough to the spanish word estupido

C – Juan ran out to the hall and into the boys' **lavatory**. He could translate the word "stupid." It was close enough to the Spanish word "estupido." (*estoopeedoh*)

26. odoriferous

No paragraph – same subject, narrator still speaking

Type of sentence – complex (subordinate clause at the end)

Commas – three adverbs together (there/in...bathroom/before lunch); noun series

Verb tense – "hid" is past tense of verb "to hide"; "came" is past tense of "to come"; and "took" is past tense of "to take"

Spelling rules – homophones (there/their/they're); compound word

Other skills – strong verb practice; possessive of plural noun

B – he hid their in the **odoriferous** boys bathroom until just before lunch when _____

_____ and _____ came in and took him back to the classroom

C – He hid there, in the **odoriferous** boys' bathroom, until just before lunch when _____,

_____, and _____ came in and took him back to the classroom.

---

27. concealed, lavatory, faced, dire, dilemmas

Paragraph – new subject (note subordinate clause as transition)

Type of sentence – complex (subordinate clause at beginning)

Commas – subordinate clause at beginning

Verb tense – add "ed" to end of regular verbs to put in past tense

Spelling rules – compound word (himself)

Other skills – reflexive pronoun incorrectly spelled (very common); possessive of plural noun; possessive pronoun (her)

Literary device – alliteration (d, d)

B – while juan **concealed** hisself in the boys **lavatory** marie **faced** some **dire dilemmas** of her own

C –   While Juan **concealed** himself in the boys' **lavatory**, Marie **faced** some **dire dilemmas** of her own.

---

28. comprehend

No paragraph – same topic, narrator still speaking

Type of sentence – simple

Punctuation – exclamation mark needed after exclamation

Commas – repeating word ("kids, kids"); appositive (extra information about a noun)

Verb tense – switch to present tense for narrator aside to the reader; correct use of conditional tense (would) as something that has not yet happened;

Other skills – who/whom/that ("who" is subject; "whom" is object of verb; "that" can be either but never should refer to people); negative

Literary devices – narrator aside; anadiplosis (repeating a word for emphasis)

B – imagine what it would be like in a room full of kids kids whom you could not **comprehend**

C – Imagine what it would be like in a room full of kids, kids whom you could not **comprehend**!

29. apprehensive

NO PARAGRAPH – narrator still speaking, same subject
TYPES OF SENTENCES – simple (compound object); simple question
PUNCTUATION – need for exclamation mark; need for question mark in question
COMMAS – noun series
VERB TENSE – switch to present tense for narrator aside; correct use of conditional tense (see note after
    Caught'ya #13); note use of infinitive "to read"
OTHER SKILL – negatives (do not use double negative)
LITERARY DEVICE – narrator aside

B – imagine what it would be like not even to be able to read no signs books or posters on the walls.
    would you be **apprehensive**

C – Imagine what it would be like not even to be able to read any signs, books, or posters on the walls!
    Would you be **apprehensive**?

---

30. apprehensive, comprehend

PARAGRAPH – same topic (apprehension) but now about Marie (new subject)
TYPES OF SENTENCES – simple; simple (compound subject); compound
COMMAS – noun series; compound sentence; repeated word
VERB TENSE – add "ed" to end of regular verbs to put in past tense; "was" is past tense of irregular verb "to be"
SPELLING RULE – "a lot" is two words
OTHER SKILLS – strong verb practice; do not begin a sentence with a conjunction (FANBOYS); review FANBOYS
LITERARY DEVICE – anadiplosis

B – marie was **apprehensive**. _____ _____ _____ _____
    and all the others looked like nice girls and boys. and they smiled at her but they asked marie a lot of
    questions questions marie could not **comprehend**

C –   Marie was **apprehensive**. _____, _____, _____, _____,
    and all the others looked like nice girls and boys. They smiled at her, but they asked Marie a lot of
    questions, questions Marie could not **comprehend**.

> **NOTE:** *After this point, a subordinate clause at the beginning or end of a complex sentence will not
> be noted. You, however, might want to look for the subordinating conjunctions and insist that your
> students never put a comma before one. (See* **Grammar, Usage, and Mechanics Guide.***)*

31. peers

NO PARAGRAPH – same subject, same speaker

TYPE OF SENTENCE – compound/complex

COMMAS – compound part of compound/complex sentence

VERB TENSE – add "ed" to end of regular verbs to put in past tense; "knew" is past tense of irregular verb "to know"; "rose" is past tense of verb "to rise"

SPELLING RULE – homophones (gnu/new/knew)

PLURAL VS. POSSESSIVE – all plurals here, nothing owned

CONTRACTIONS – "couldn't" means "could not"

OTHER SKILLS – strong verb practice; negative (no double negatives like "couldn't not"); review FANBOYS

B – marie knew her **peers** were asking questions because there voices rose at the end of each sentence but she couldnt not understand what they asked

C – Marie knew her **peers** were asking questions because their voices rose at the end of each sentence, but she couldn't understand what they asked.

> **NOTE:** *Third-graders are not yet ready to learn about transitive and intransitive verbs (rise vs. raise, sit vs. set, lie vs. lay), but they do need to know when to use each correctly. Just model them correctly, and gently correct your students when they make an error. You could try to illustrate using kinesthetic techniques (raise the chair, rise up yourself, etc.). Leave the more complicated explanations for middle-school teachers to struggle with.*

---

32. exasperation

PARAGRAPH – new person speaking

TYPES OF SENTENCES – simple; simple (in French); simple

CAPITALIZATION – always capitalize "I" since each person is important; always capitalize the first letter in a quote unless it is a continued quote; always capitalize the names of countries and languages

PUNCTUATION – use of quotation marks around what is said out loud; question mark needed after question (even in French)

COMMAS – introductory adverb; before quote; before and after quote

VERB TENSE – add "ed" to end of regular verbs to put in past tense; "said" is past tense of irregular verb "to say"; "meant" is past tense of verb "to mean"; switch to present tense for quote

SPELLING RULE – common error (double the "L" in "finally")

OTHER SKILL – strong verb practice

B – finally she said in **exasperation** quoi? je ne vous comprends pas. in french this meant what i do not understand you

C – Finally, she said in **exasperation**, "Quoi? Je ne vous comprends pas." In French this meant, "What? I do not understand you." (***Kwoah? juh nuh voo caw praw pah." Do not pronounce the "nt." It is a nasal sound in French.***)

33. perplexed, apprehensive

3 PARAGRAPHS – new persons speaking
TYPES OF SENTENCES – simple; compound; simple
CAPITALIZATION – always capitalize "I"
PUNCTUATION – use of quotation marks around what is said out loud
COMMAS – quote; compound sentence; quote; quote
VERB TENSE – "said" is past tense of irregular verb "to say"; switch to present tense for quote
SPELLING RULE – homophones (know/no)
CONTRACTIONS – "we've" = we have; don't = do not
OTHER SKILLS – negatives; review FANBOYS
LITERARY DEVICE – conversation

B – i think weve **perplexed** her said _____. i dont know what marie said but she looks **apprehensive** said _____. i agree said _____

C –   "I think we've **perplexed** her," said _____.
        "I don't know what Marie said, but she looks **apprehensive**," said _____.
        "I agree," said _____.

34. queried

PARAGRAPH – new person speaking
TYPE OF SENTENCE – simple quote
PUNCTUATION – use of quotation marks around what is said out loud; question mark needed after question
COMMA – relative pronoun clause (who)
VERB TENSE – add "ed" to most verbs to form past tense; "was" is past tense of irregular verb "to be"; switch to present tense for quote
OTHER SKILL – relative pronouns (who = subject; whom = object; that = both, but never for a person)

B – what can we do **queried** _____ who always was concerned about the feelings of others

C –   "What can we do?" **queried** _____, who always was concerned about the feelings of others.

35. queries, agreed

2 PARAGRAPHS – two persons speaking
TYPES OF SENTENCES – simple; deliberate fragment; simple question
CAPITALIZATION – always capitalize the beginning of quotes except in a continued quote (one interrupted by the information about who said it); always capitalize the names of languages
PUNCTUATION – use of quotation marks around what is said out loud; question mark after question
COMMAS – end of quote; after interjection and quote; after interrupter of quote before quote picks up again
VERB TENSE – add "ed" to end of regular verbs to put in past tense; switch to present tense for quote
CONTRACTION – "let's" = let us
OTHER SKILL – strong verb practice
LITERARY DEVICE – use of slang word ("yeah")

B – lets stop making **queries** suggested _____. yeah **agreed** _____ why don't we teach her some words in english

C –   "Let's stop making **queries**," suggested _____.
        "Yeah," **agreed** _____. "Why don't we teach her some words in English?"

36. lectern

PARAGRAPH – new person speaking (narrator)

TYPES OF SENTENCES – simple; simple (compound objects)

CAPITALIZATION – always capitalize the names of languages; do not capitalize the names of subjects unless it is a language (English)

COMMAS – introductory word; interrupter (extra information); noun list

VERB TENSE – "taught" is past tense of irregular verb "to teach"

SPELLING RULES – compound word; commonly misspelled word "a lot" is two words; difficult word "taught"

OTHER SKILLS – strong verb practice; use of colon before a long list (please note that a colon never follows a verb)

B – well for the rest of the morning instead of language arts the class taught marie a lot of english nouns. they taught her the following words: girl boy teacher desk **lectern** blackboard chalk window paper pencil book and eraser

C –   Well, for the rest of the morning, instead of language arts, the class taught Marie a lot of English nouns. They taught her the following words: girl, boy, teacher, desk, **lectern**, blackboard, chalk, window, paper, pencil, book, and eraser.

> **NOTE:** *Third-graders are not yet ready to use colons on their own. Therefore, I would suggest leaving the colon in when you put this Caught'ya on the board, but point it out so that students can eventually learn the concept. Also you will want to point out that a colon never follows a verb. This might sink in for later retrieval in fifth grade.*

37. renowned

> **NOTE:** *I'm sure that you are familiar with the French song, "Frère Jacques" ("Brother John"). If not, chances are someone at your school knows the tune. Here are the words, first in French, then in English, and then phonetically. There are many recordings of this in record shops. You may find that most of your children already know the song (sort of).*

"Frère Jacques"
Frère Jacques, Frère Jacques,
Dormez-vous? Dormez-vous?
Sonnez les matines. Sonnez les matines.
Din, din, don. Din, din, don.

"Brother John"
Brother John, Brother John,
Are you sleeping? Are you sleeping?
Ring the morning bells. Ring the morning bells.
Ding, ding, dong. Ding, ding, dong.

Pronunciation
Frayreh Jah-keh, Frayreh Jah-keh,
Dormay-voo? Dormay-voo?
Sonnay lay mateeneh. Sonnay lay mateeneh.
Dahn, dahn, dohn. Dahn, dahn, dohn.
(*Make it nasal-sounding*)

PARAGRAPH – new subject

TYPES OF SENTENCES – simple; simple question

CAPITALIZATION – capitalize names of songs and languages

PUNCTUATION – use of quotation marks around name of song (album would be underlined)

COMMAS – introductory adverb; 2 adjectives without "and" in between

VERB TENSE – "taught" is past tense of verb "to teach"; switch to present tense for narrator aside

SPELLING RULE – difficult word "taught"

OTHER SKILLS – strong verb practice; use of parentheses for narrator aside when you step out of the story; note use of hyphen for two words acting as one

LITERARY DEVICE – narrator aside in parentheses

B – in return marie taught her new class to sing the old well-known song frère jacques. (can you sing that **renowned** french song)

C – In return, Marie taught her new class to sing the old, well-known song "Frère Jacques." (***Frayreh Jah-keh***) (Can you sing that **renowned** French song?)

NOTE #1: *I suggest that you leave in the parentheses for modeling. This is a powerful tool, but young children can overuse it. Point out the parentheses and the reason for them, but I wouldn't dwell on them. Personally, I overuse parentheses (just love them) all the time. You do not want your students to develop this bad habit.*

NOTE #2: *Point out the accent in the French word "frère." You simply can tell your students how lucky they are to be speaking and writing English where there are no accents. Most other languages have them, and they count in spelling tests!*

---

38. peers

NO PARAGRAPH – same topic

TYPES OF SENTENCES – simple; complex

CAPITALIZATION – capitalize names of languages

COMMAS – always surround "too" with commas when it means "also"; introductory phrase

VERB TENSE – "taught" is past tense of verb "to teach"; "knew" is past tense of verb "to know"

SPELLING RULES – homophones (to/too/two and gnu/knew/new); difficult word "taught"

OTHER SKILLS – strong verb practice; negatives (no double negatives in English)

B – marie taught her **peers** a few words in french too. of course she taught them by pointing since she didn't know no english

C – Marie taught her **peers** a few words in French, too. Of course, she taught them by pointing since she knew no English.

39. camaraderie

No paragraph – same topic

Type of sentence – simple (compound object)

Capitalization – always capitalize the names of languages

Commas – introductory phrase; noun series

Verb tense – "taught" is past tense of verb "to teach"

Other skills – strong verb practice; use of colon before long series (never use colon after a verb); use of parentheses around translation (extra information)

B – in **camaraderie** marie taught her new friends the following words in french: le garçon (the boy) la fille (the girl) le crayon (the pencil) and mon livre (my book)

C – In **camaraderie**, Marie taught her new friends the following words in French: le garçon (the boy) (*luh garsaunh—do not pronounce the "n" as it is nasal*), la fille (the girl) (*lah feeyuh*), le crayon (the pencil) (*luh crayaunh—do not pronounce the "n"*), and mon livre (my book) (*maunh leevruh—do not pronounce the "n"*).

> **NOTE:** *Point out accent in French for which French children are responsible on their spelling tests!*

---

40. brief, respite

Paragraph – new time and topic

Type of sentence – simple; complex

Punctuation – use of quotation marks around what is said out loud

Commas – noun series; subordinate clause at beginning of sentence

Verb tense – add "ed" to end of regular verbs to put in past tense; pluperfect ("had been sent")

Spelling rules – consonant/vowel/consonant = double 2nd consonant when adding suffix

Plural vs. possessive – use of plural and singular possessive (go over rules)

Other skills – strong verb practice; review preposition use (before, for, from)

B – _____ _____ and _____ had been sent to find juan. when they all returned from the boys lavatory just before lunch the class stopped for a **brief respite** from the mornings work

C – _____, _____, and _____ had been sent to find Juan. When they all returned from the boys' lavatory just before lunch, the class stopped for a **brief respite** from the morning's work.

41. devoured, equipment

NO PARAGRAPH – same topic (details)

TYPE OF SENTENCE – simple (compound verb)

PUNCTUATION – use of quotation marks around words used out of context

COMMAS – verb series

VERB TENSE – add "ed" to end of regular verbs to put in past tense; "went" is past tense of irregular verb "to go"; "taught" is past tense of verb "to teach"

SPELLING RULE – compound words (playground, outdoor)

OTHER SKILL – strong verb practice

B – they **devoured** lunch went out to the playground played on the **equipment** visited with each other and taught juan and marie outdoor words like "tree" and "sky"

C – They **devoured** lunch, went out to the playground, played on the **equipment**, visited with each other, and taught Juan and Marie outdoor words like "tree" and "sky."

---

42. putrescent

PARAGRAPH – new topic

TYPE OF SENTENCE – compound

COMMAS – two adjectives not separated by "and" where second is not age, size, or linked to noun; compound sentence

VERB TENSE – "was" is past tense of irregular verb "to be"; "felt" is past tense of verb "to feel"

SPELLING RULES – difficult word "beautiful"; compound word; consonant/vowel/consonant + suffix = double 2nd consonant (sunny)

OTHER SKILLS – comparatives (good/better/best); review FANBOYS

B – it was a beautiful sunny day and juan felt better to be out of the **putrescent** bathroom

C – It was a beautiful, sunny day, and Juan felt better to be out of the **putrescent** bathroom.

---

43. azure, shrilly

NO PARAGRAPH – same topic (details)

TYPES OF SENTENCES – simple; complex

VERB TENSE – add "ed" to end of regular verbs to put in past tense; "flew" is past tense of irregular verb "to fly"

SPELLING RULES – most plurals are formed by adding "s"; homophones (flew/flu); compound word

OTHER SKILL – strong verb practice

LITERARY DEVICES – strong verb description; alliteration (f, f)

B – a few fluffy clouds floated across the **azure** sky. birds chirped **shrilly** as they flew overhead

C – A few fluffy clouds floated across the **azure** sky. Birds chirped **shrilly** as they flew overhead.

44. cavorted

No paragraph – same topic (details)

Type of sentence – simple (compound verb)

Verb tense – add "ed" to end of regular verbs to put in past tense

Spelling rule – difficult word "squirrel"

Other skill – strong verb practice

Literary devices – strong verb description; personification (making a thing—the tree—do a human act); metaphor (arms for branches)

B – squirrels played and **cavorted** on the trunks and branches of oak trees that spread their wide arms towards the sky

C – Squirrels played and **cavorted** on the trunks and branches of oak trees that spread their wide arms towards the sky.

45. chattered, faintly

No paragraph – same topic (the description)

Types of sentences – both simple

Capitalization – always capitalize the first letter of a quote

Punctuation – use of quotation marks around what is said out loud

Commas – long introductory adverb (really two adverbs); before quote

Verb tense – add "ed" to end of regular verbs to put in past tense

Possessive – use of plural possessive in word that does not end in "s"

Other skill – strong verb practice

Literary device – strong verb description

Onomatopoeia – word that represents a sound ("beep")

B – happy childrens voices **chattered** all around juan. somewhere in the distance a car horn tooted **faintly** beep. beep

C – Happy children's voices **chattered** all around Juan. Somewhere in the distance, a car horn tooted **faintly**, "Beep. Beep."

46. embarrassment

No paragraph – same topic

Types of sentences – simple; simple (compound verb)

Comma – repeating word

Verb tense – add "ed" to end of regular verbs to put in past tense; "was" is past tense of irregular verb "to be"; "forgot" is past tense of verb "to forget"

Spelling rule – difficult word "beautiful"

Other skills – comparatives (good/better/best); never begin a sentence with a conjunction (see note with Caught'ya #9); possessive pronoun "his"

B – it was a beautiful day a day that would make anyone feel better. and juan breathed deeply and forgot his **embarrassment**

C – It was a beautiful day, a day that would make anyone feel better. Juan breathed deeply and forgot his **embarrassment**.

> NOTE: *This might be a good place to teach simple possessive pronouns (my, your, his, her, its, our, their).*

47. firm

Paragraph – new time

Type of sentence – compound

Commas – introductory adverb; compound sentence; two adjectives not separated by "and" where 2nd adjective is not age, color, or linked to noun

Verb tense – "was" is past tense of irregular verb "to be"; "had" is past tense of verb "to have"; "made" is past tense of verb "to make"; use of pluperfect tense (had made) to denote action that took place previous to this sentence

Spelling rule – homophones (gnu, new, knew)

Other skills – note hyphen between two words used as one; review FANBOYS

Literary device – alliteration ("firm friends")

B – too soon it was time to go inside but juan and marie had made **firm** friends in their new third-grade class

C – Too soon, it was time to go inside, but Juan and Marie had made **firm** friends in their new, third-grade class.

48. shrill

2 PARAGRAPHS – new subjects referred to (teacher and whistle); quote

TYPES OF SENTENCES – both simple quotes

CAPITALIZATION – always capitalize the first letter of a quote unless it is a continuation

PUNCTUATION – use of quotation marks around what is said out loud

COMMAS – appositive (extra information about a noun); before quote; after quote

VERB TENSE – "blew" is past tense of verb "to blow"; switch to present tense for quote

SPELLING RULE – homophones (its/it's)

OTHER SKILLS – never begin a sentence with a conjunction (FANBOYS); review FANBOYS; go over preposition use; abbreviations of titles (Mr., Ms., Miss, or Mrs. before the teacher's name)

LITERARY DEVICE – onomatopoeia (word mimicking sound)

B – and the teacher _____ blew a **shrill** whistle tweeeet. its time to go in she said

C – The teacher, _____, blew a **shrill** whistle, "Tweeeet."
"It's time to go in," she said.

---

49. docile, dormice

PARAGRAPH – new person speaking (narrator)

TYPE OF SENTENCE – simple

COMMAS – extra information (FYI – participial phrase)

VERB TENSE – add "ed" to end of regular verbs to put in past tense

SPELLING RULES – homophones (hole/whole); unusual plural of "mouse"

OTHER SKILLS – strong verb practice

LITERARY DEVICE – simile

B – the hole class including juan and marie lined up at the door as quiet and **docile** as **dormice**

C – The whole class, including Juan and Marie, lined up at the door as quiet and **docile** as **dormice**.

---

50. uneventfully, peers

PARAGRAPH – new time

TYPES OF SENTENCES – simple; compound

CAPITALIZATION – always capitalize the names of languages

COMMA – compound sentence

VERB TENSE – add "ed" to end of regular verbs to put in past tense; "taught" is past tense of irregular verb "to teach"

OTHER SKILLS – strong verb practice; review FANBOYS

B – the rest of the day passed **uneventfully**. juan and marie learned even more english and they taught some french and spanish to their **peers** in return

C – The rest of the day passed **uneventfully**. Juan and Marie learned even more English, and they taught some French and Spanish to their **peers** in return.

51. inventively, instruct

No PARAGRAPH – same topic, same time

TYPES OF SENTENCES – simple (compound subject); simple

PUNCTUATION – use of quotation marks around words used out of context; note periods and commas always go inside quotes

COMMAS – noun series; noun series

VERB TENSE – add "ed" to end of regular verbs to put in past tense

SPELLING RULE – homophones (their/there/they're)

OTHER SKILL – strong verb practice

LITERARY DEVICES – simile with "like" (used for direct noun comparison only); alliteration (i, i, i)

B – _____ _____ _____ and _____ pointed out more nouns like "pig" "dog" and "cat." they **inventively** used drawings in there reading books to **instruct** the foreign students

C – _____, _____, _____, and _____ pointed out more nouns like "pig," "dog," and "cat." They **inventively** used drawings in their reading books to **instruct** the foreign students.

> NOTE: *If you feel that your students can handle it, take out the quotation marks around "pig," "dog," and "cat" in the board version. They have seen this rule several times now.*

---

52. expanding, adjectives

No PARAGRAPH – same time, same topic, same place

TYPES OF SENTENCES – simple; simple (compound object)

PUNCTUATION – use of quotation marks around words out of context

COMMAS – always surround "too" with commas if it means "also"

VERB TENSE – add "ed" to end of regular verbs to put in past tense; "taught" is past tense of irregular verb "to teach"

SPELLING RULE – homophones (their/there/they're)

OTHER SKILLS – inform students of use of dash; strong verb practice; go over adverbs and adjectives

B – the teacher introduced a verb into their already **expanding** vocabulary—"to be." she taught juan and marie a few **adjectives** too

C – The teacher introduced a verb into their already **expanding** vocabulary—"to be." She taught Juan and Marie a few **adjectives**, too.

> NOTE: *This would be a good place to introduce the eight parts of speech: nouns, interjections, prepositions, pronouns, adverbs, verbs, adjectives, conjunctions (NIPPAVAC). See the note in the* **Grammar, Usage, and Mechanics Guide** *on the parts of speech. A mini-lesson on adverbs and adjectives might be appropriate here.*

53. adjective

NOTE: *Use your name here so that you can discuss abbreviations of titles.*

PARAGRAPH – narrator aside to reader

TYPES OF SENTENCES – all simple questions

PUNCTUATION – question marks needed after questions

VERB TENSE – switch to present tense for narrator aside

SPELLING RULE – most words become plural by adding "s"

OTHER SKILLS – use article (adjective) "an" before a word that begins with a vowel; abbreviation of your title (Mr., Ms., Miss, or Mrs.)

LITERARY DEVICE – narrator aside

B – what is an **adjective**? can you name a few of them? what adjectives do you think _____ taught juan and marie

C – What is an **adjective**? Can you name a few of them? What adjectives do you think _____ taught Juan and Marie?

---

54. utter

PARAGRAPH – new time

TYPE OF SENTENCE – compound/complex

CAPITALIZATION – always capitalize the name of a language

COMMA – compound/complex sentence

VERB TENSE – "could" is past tense of irregular verb "can"; "knew" is past tense of verb "to know"

SPELLING RULE – homophones (gnu/new/knew)

OTHER SKILLS – "fewer" can be counted, and "less" refers to vague things that cannot be counted ("fewer people" can be counted, but "less active" is a concept and can't be counted); difference between "then" (adverb) and "than" (comparative); write out numbers to 121

B – by the end of the day juan and marie could **utter** a few more things in english although they still knew fewer than fifty words in all and they new only 1 verb

C – By the end of the day Juan and Marie could **utter** a few more things in English although they still knew fewer than fifty words in all, and they knew only one verb.

55. foreign, lavatory

PARAGRAPH – time change, subject change

TYPES OF SENTENCES – both simple

PUNCTUATION – use of exclamation mark in exclamation

COMMA – long introductory adverb

VERB TENSE – "could" is past tense of irregular verb "can"

SPELLING RULE – "i" before "e" except after "c," and "**n**e**i**ghbor," "**w**e**i**gh," and "the**i**r" are "**w**e**i**rd"

OTHER SKILLS – write out numbers to 121; hyphen between 2 words acting as 1

B – by the end of the week the 2 **foreign** third-graders could say a few sentences. now juan could read the words on the **lavatory** doors

C –   By the end of the week, the two **foreign** third-graders could say a few sentences. Now Juan could read the words on the **lavatory** doors!

---

56. vocalize

NOTE: Translation in next Caught'ya...

PARAGRAPH – new people introduced

TYPES OF SENTENCES– both simple (compound objects)

CAPITALIZATION – always capitalize the first letter of a quote unless it is a continuation (even in French and Spanish)

PUNCTUATION – use of quotation marks around what is said out loud

COMMAS – before quotes and after quote

VERB TENSE – "knew" is past tense of irregular verb "to know"; "could" is past tense of verb "can"

SPELLING RULE – homophones (gnu/new/knew)

B – the rest of the class also new a few sentences in french and spanish. they could **vocalize** tu es un cochon moche in french and tu es un cerdo feo in spanish

C –   The rest of the class also knew a few sentences in French and Spanish. They could **vocalize** "Tu es un cochon moche" in French and "Tu es uno cerdo feo" in Spanish. (*Too eh unh coshaunhy mohsch and Too ess oono serdo fayoh*)

57. affront

No paragraph – continuation
Types of sentences – simple; simple (compound verb)
Capitalization – always capitalize the first letter of a quote unless it is a continuation
Punctuation – use of quotation marks around what is said out loud
Commas – before quote; note no comma before "and" as it is not a compound sentence (no subject), only a compound verb
Verb tense – "meant" is past tense of verb "to mean"; "could" is past tense of verb "can"; switch to present tense for quote
Spelling rules – homophones (their/there/they're); form plural of nouns that end in consonant "y" by replacing "y" with "ies" (enemy/enemies)
Other skills – article (adjective) "an" must be used before word that begins with a vowel or a silent "h"; hyphen between 2 words acting as 1

B – both meant you are an ugly pig. now the third-graders could tease their friends and insult and **affront** there enemies

C – Both meant, "You are an ugly pig." Now the third-graders could tease their friends and insult and **affront** their enemies.

---

58. peers

Paragraph – new time
Types of sentences – simple; simple (compound object)
Capitalization – always capitalize the name of a language
Verb tense – add "ed" to end of regular verbs to put in past tense; "went" is past tense of irregular verb "to go"
Spelling rule – homophones (there/their/they're)
Other skills – strong verb practice; review simple possessive pronouns (my, your, his, her, our, their)

B – weeks went by. marie and juan learned more and more english from there teacher and from their **peers**

C –   Weeks went by. Marie and Juan learned more and more English from their teacher and from their **peers**.

---

59. a plethora of

No paragraph – same topic
Types of sentences – simple; complex
Capitalization – always capitalize the name of a language
Commas – interrupter
Verb tense – "could" is past tense of irregular verb "can"; "made" is past tense of verb "to make"; "spoke" is past tense of verb "to speak"
Spelling rule – "a lot" is two words (meaning of vocabulary word)
Other skill – strong verb practice

B – they could now speak in sentences. they still made **a plethora of** mistakes though when they spoke english

C – They could now speak in sentences. They still made **a plethora of** mistakes, though, when they spoke English.

60. prepositions

PARAGRAPH – now about Marie

TYPE OF SENTENCE – simple

VERB TENSE – "could" is past tense of irregular verb "can"

SPELLING RULE – homophones (straight/strait)

OTHER SKILLS – never split verb parts or infinitives (*Star Trek's* "to boldly go" was wrong.); negatives

B – marie could never get the **prepositions** straight

C – Marie never could get the **prepositions** straight.

> **NOTE:** *Now that it is halfway through the year, you might want to find a list of prepositions (in the* **Grammar, Usage, and Mechanics Guide**) *and begin to have your students memorize them. This is a useful tool. Once young students have memorized the prepositions, it is easy to tell them not to capitalize them in a title. Prepositional phrases (simple phrases acting as adjectives and adverbs) can be understood and correctly used when a future teacher asks students to use more adjectives or adverbs to flesh out a story or essay. When the prepositions have been memorized, have your students recite them whenever one occurs in a subsequent Caught'ya. Again, you will be very popular with the teachers who come after you. Note that I have not identified prepositions for the teachers to the left of each Caught'ya.*

61. identical

NO PARAGRAPH – same topic (details)

TYPE OF SENTENCE – compound with semicolon

CAPITALIZATION – capitalize names of languages

PUNCTUATION – use of quotation marks around words out of context (I suggest taking out every other one as I did to challenge your students.); note that commas and periods always go inside quotes

VERB TENSE – "said" is past tense of verb "to say"; "were" is past tense of irregular verb "to be"

OTHER SKILLS – use of semicolon instead of FANBOYS in a compound sentence; avoidance of direct quote by using "that"

B – she said that she "walked of home at school" instead of walked from home to school because "from" and of in french were **identical** words; so were "at" and to

C – She said that she "walked of home at school" instead of "walked from home to school" because "from" and "of" in French are **identical** words; so are "at" and "to."

62. persisted

NO PARAGRAPH – same topic

TYPES OF SENTENCES – complex; simple (compound object)

CAPITALIZATION – always capitalize names of languages

PUNCTUATION – use of quotation marks around words that are out of context; note that all periods and commas go inside quotes

COMMA – subordinate clause at beginning

VERB TENSE – add "ed" to end of regular verbs to put in past tense; "had" is past tense of irregular verb "to have"; use of present tense for truism ("Because the French place…")

OTHER SKILL – article (adjective) "an" must be used before a vowel or a silent "h"

B – because the french place most adjectives after the noun marie had a hard time with adjectives. she **persisted** in saying "a pig ugly" instead of an ugly pig

C – Because the French place most adjectives after the noun, Marie had a hard time with adjectives. She **persisted** in saying "a pig ugly" instead of "an ugly pig."

---

63. predicament

PARAGRAPH – new topic (Juan)

TYPES OF SENTENCES – both simple

CAPITALIZATION – always capitalize the name of a language

COMMAS – interrupter

VERB TENSE – "had" is past tense of irregular verb "to have"; switch to present tense for truism

SPELLING RULE – homophones (their/there/they're)

B – juan on the other hand had a **predicament** with verbs. in spanish their are 2 verbs for "is"

C – Juan, on the other hand, had a **predicament** with verbs. In Spanish there are two verbs for "is."

> **NOTE:** *Now that we are halfway through the Caught'yas, I shall no longer list the need to capitalize the names of countries and languages.*

---

64. pronunciation

NO PARAGRAPH – same topic, same person

TYPES OF SENTENCES – both simple

CAPITALIZATION – always capitalize the first letter of a quote unless it is a continuation; always capitalize "I"

PUNCTUATION – use of quotation marks around what is said out loud

COMMA – before quote

VERB TENSE – "said" is past tense of verb "to say"; "had" is past tense of irregular verb "to have"

OTHER SKILLS – review prepositions; correct form of the verb "to be"

B – sometimes he said "i is ready" instead of i am ready. he also had trouble with **pronunciation**

C – Sometimes he said "I is ready" instead of "I am ready." He also had trouble with **pronunciation**.

65. amusing, foreign

PARAGRAPH – new topic

TYPE OF SENTENCE – complex

COMMAS – subordinate clause at beginning; extra information about "class"; appositive

VERB TENSE – add "ed" to end of regular verbs to put in past tense; "was" is past tense of irregular verb "to be"

PLURAL VS. POSSESSIVE – possessive of singular noun

OTHER SKILLS – abbreviations (in the title of your name); hyphen in two words acting as one adjective; teach ordinal numbers (first, second, third, fourth, etc.); write out numbers to 121; begin to teach collective pronouns like "everyone" and "everybody" and collective nouns like "class" that take singular form of verb and singular modifiers

B – since everyone was included in the language lessons everybody in _____s third-grade class including the teacher learned a few **amusing** words and sentences in two **foreign** languages french and spanish

C – Since everyone was included in the language lessons, everybody in _____'s third-grade class, including the teacher, learned a few **amusing** words and sentences in two **foreign** languages, French and Spanish.

---

66. keen, intelligent, attempted

NOTE: *Translation in the next Caught'ya...*

NO PARAGRAPH – same topic because quotes are indirect

TYPES OF SENTENCES – both simple

CAPITALIZATION – always capitalize the first letter of a quote unless it is a continuation

PUNCTUATION – use of quotation marks around what is said out loud

COMMAS – two adjectives where the 2nd adjective is not age, color, or linked to noun; before and after quotes

VERB TENSE – add "ed" to end of regular verbs to put in past tense

OTHER SKILLS – note use of infinitives; strong verb practice

B – the **keen intelligent** class learned to say yo soy superfino in spanish. they **attempted** to say je suis formidable in french

C – The **keen, intelligent** class learned to say "Yo soy superfino" in Spanish. They **attempted** to say "Je suis formidable" in French. (*Yo soy soupearfeeeno; Juh swee formidaaaabluh*)

---

67. expressions, respective

NO PARAGRAPH – continuation

TYPE OF SENTENCE – simple

CAPITALIZATION – always capitalize the first letter of a quote unless it is a continuation; always capitalize "I"

PUNCTUATION – use of quotation marks around what is said out loud

COMMAS – before and after quote

VERB TENSE – "meant" is past tense of irregular verb "to mean"; switch to present tense for quote

SPELLING RULE – homophones (to/two/too and their/they're/there)

OTHER SKILLS – write out numbers to 121; go over adjectives "this," "that," "these," and "those"

B – those 2 **expressions** meant i am super in their **respective** languages

C – Those two **expressions** meant, "I am super," in their **respective** languages.

68. severe

No paragraph – continuation

Types of sentences – both simple quotes

Capitalization – always capitalize the first letter of a quote even in French

Punctuation – use of quotation marks around what is said out loud; quotes needed around idiomatic expression; note quote within a quote, and point it out to your students

Commas – before and after quote; before quote

Verb tense – add "ed" to end of regular verbs to put in past tense; "meant" is past tense of irregular verb "to mean"; switch to present tense for quote

Plural vs. possessive – possessive of singular noun

Literary device – use of idiomatic expression

B – the class also learned to say tu es un casse-pied in maries language. this meant you are a **severe** 'pain in the neck'

C – The class also learned to say, "Tu es uncasse-pied" (*too eh cahss pee-ay*) in Marie's language. This meant, "You are a **severe** 'pain in the neck.'"

---

69. declare

NOTE: *Translation in the next Caught'ya...*

Paragraph – same topic but new expression being taught by new person

Type of sentence – simple quote

Capitalization – always capitalize the first letter of a quote even in French

Punctuation – use of quotation marks around what is said out loud

Commas – before quote

Verb tense – "taught" is past tense of irregular verb "to teach"

Spelling rules – difficult word "taught"

B – juan taught the class to **declare** "eres una lata

C – Juan taught the class to **declare**, "Eres una lata." (*Eyres oona lahtah—accent on first syllable in all words*)

70. expression

PARAGRAPH – new subject

TYPE OF SENTENCE – complex

CAPITALIZATION – always capitalize the first letter of a quote unless it is a continuation

PUNCTUATION – use of quotation marks around what is said out loud

COMMAS – interrupter; before quote

VERB TENSE – add "ed" to end of regular verbs to put in past tense; "did" is past tense of irregular verb "to do"; switch to present tense for quote

OTHER SKILLS – negative; use of parentheses for aside (Note that I have put in the first one for the students. They can probably figure out that there must be a second at the end of the phrase.)

B – the teacher however did not like this **expression** (even though it was in spanish because it had almost the same meaning as you are a pain in the rear

C –   The teacher, however, did not like this **expression** (even though it was in Spanish) because it had almost the same meaning as, "You are a pain in the rear."

---

71. whispered, murmured

NO PARAGRAPH – continuation

TYPE OF SENTENCE – complex

VERB TENSE – add "ed" to end of regular verbs to put in past tense; "thought" is past tense of irregular verb "to think"

SPELLING RULE – note correct spelling of "themselves" if your students spell this word incorrectly (theirselves)

OTHER SKILLS – strong verb practice; "between" refers to only two things or people while "among" refers to more than two; negative; teach object pronouns (me, you, him, her, us, them)

B – the class **whispered** and **murmured** it among themselves when they thought the teacher could not hear them

C – The class **whispered** and **murmured** it among themselves when they thought the teacher could not hear them.

---

72. exemplary

NO PARAGRAPH – continuation

TYPE OF SENTENCE – complex

COMMAS – interrupter

VERB TENSE – "could" is past tense of irregular verb "can"; switch to present tense for truism

SPELLING RULE – homophones (here/hear)

B – she could hear them of course because teachers always have **exemplary** hearing

C – She could hear them, of course, because teachers always have **exemplary** hearing.

73. **challenging, prove**

PARAGRAPH – new topic

TYPES OF SENTENCES – simple; compound

PUNCTUATION – exclamation mark needed in exclamation

COMMA – compound sentence

VERB TENSE – "was" is past tense of irregular verb "to be"; correct use of conditional tense (to denote something that might happen)

SPELLING RULES – "i" before "e" except after "c"

LITERARY DEVICE – foreshadowing to build suspense in story

B – it was fun learning words in a foreign language. it was **challenging** to teach juan and marie english but it also would **prove** to be dangerous

C –   It was fun learning words in a foreign language. It was **challenging** to teach Juan and Marie English, but it also would **prove** to be dangerous!

---

74. **concluded**

NO PARAGRAPH – same topic

TYPE OF SENTENCE – simple (compound subject)

COMMAS – noun series; introductory adverb (to independent clause); interrupter

VERB TENSE – add "ed" to end of regular verbs to put in past tense; "was" is past tense of irregular verb "to be"

OTHER SKILL – use of italics for emphasis

B – _____ _____ _____ and _____ **concluded** that so far this *was* indeed the best year yet

C – _____, _____, _____, and _____ **concluded** that so far, this *was*, indeed, the best year yet.

---

75. **appalling, ensue**

PARAGRAPH – new topic

TYPE OF SENTENCE – simple (compound object)

COMMA – use of comma for clarity and effect

VERB TENSE – "did" is past tense of verb "to do"; "were" is past tense of irregular verb "to be"

SPELLING RULES – consonant/vowel/consonant + suffix = double 2nd consonant; homophones (no/know)

OTHER SKILLS – "between" refers to only two people or things, "among" refers to more than two

LITERARY DEVICE – foreshadowing to build suspense

B – they did not know the **appalling** problems that were about to **ensue** among them and the fifth grade all because of language problems

C –   They did not know the **appalling** problems that were about to **ensue** between them and the fifth grade, all because of language problems.

76. brisk

PARAGRAPH – new time and subject

TYPES OF SENTENCES – both simple

VERB TENSE – "was" is past tense of irregular verb "to be"; "began" is past tense of verb "to begin"

SPELLING RULES – compound word; homophones (won/one)

OTHER SKILL – teach the use of "very" as an adverb that can tell you more about a verb, an adjective, or another adverb

LITERARY DEVICE – foreshadowing

B – it all began on the playground one **brisk** winter day. juan was very excited

C –   It all began on the playground one **brisk** winter day. Juan was very excited.

77. cronies

NO PARAGRAPH – same topic

TYPES OF SENTENCES – compound; complex (sub. clause at end)

CAPITALIZATION – always capitalize the first letter of months, days, and holidays

COMMAS – date, appositive (extra information about a noun); two adjectives where the 2nd is not age, color, or linked to noun

VERB TENSE – "was" is past tense of irregular verb "to be"

SPELLING RULE – homophones (gnu/new/knew and there/their/they're); form plural of nouns that end in consonant "y" by replacing "y" with "ics"

OTHER SKILL – teach simple subject pronouns (I, you, he, she, it we, they)

B – it was december and he was going to share the mexican tradition of Posada with his new american **cronies**. posada began on december 16th and lasted until december 24th when their were lots of big parties

C – It was December, and he was going to share the Mexican tradition of Posada with his new American **cronies**. Posada began on December 16th and lasted until December 24th when there were lots of big parties.

78. mammoth

NO PARAGRAPH – same topic

TYPES OF SENTENCES – complex; simple

PUNCTUATION – use of quotation marks around foreign word not in a quote

COMMAS – sub. clause; noun list

VERB TENSE – add "ed" to end of regular verbs to put in past tense; "had" is past tense of irregular verb "to have"

SPELLING RULE – homophones (whole/hole)

OTHER SKILL – review FANBOYS

B – in an **mammoth** box almost as big as him juan carried mexican food for the hole class a "piñata and some "buñuelos. He had studied his english to be able to tell his classmates about the custom of posada

C – In a **mammoth** box almost as big as he was, Juan carried Mexican food for the whole class, a "piñata," and some "buñuelos." He had studied his English to be able to tell his classmates about the custom of Posada. *(piñata = peenyahtah—accent on "yah;" buñuelos = bunyouwailos—accent on "whale")*

79. a plethora of, traditional

> **NOTE:** *This would be a good place to discuss and explore some American cultural traditions.*

NO PARAGRAPH – same topic (details)

TYPES OF SENTENCES – both simple

CAPITALIZATION – always capitalize the names of countries and holidays

COMMAS – none between "big chocolate" as second adjective is linked to noun like "white picket fence"; elaboration (extra information)

VERB TENSE – "had sent" is the pluperfect of the verb "to send" and is used here to indicate action that took place before this paragraph; "was" is past tense of irregular verb "to be"

SPELLING RULES – form plural of nouns that end in consonant "y" by replacing "y" with "ies"

PLURAL VS. POSSESSIVE – singular possessive noun

OTHER SKILL – use of "as" instead of "like" for comparison ("like" only compares two nouns—or pronouns— directly as in "a boy like Juan")

B – juans uncle in mexico had sent the "piñata that was filled with "dulces and little toys as well as a real "pan dulce. his mother had made **a plethora of** "buñuelos and other **traditional** goodeys for juans class just like mothers here bake cupcakes for birthday parteys

C – Juan's uncle in Mexico had sent the "piñata" that was filled with "dulces" and little toys as well as a real "pan dulce." His mother had made **a plethora of** "buñuelos" and other **traditional** goodies for Juan's class just as mothers here bake cupcakes for birthday parties. (*piñata = peenyatah; dulces = duelsayes; pan dulce = pahn duelsay; buñuelos = bunyouwailos—all accents on the second-to-last syllable*)

---

80. whistled

PARAGRAPH – new time

TYPE OF SENTENCE – complex

COMMAS – no comma as subordinate clause is at end of sentence

VERB TENSE – add "ed" to end of regular verbs to put in past tense

SPELLING RULES – compound word

OTHER SKILL – strong verb practice

LITERARY DEVICES – description; alliteration (winter, whistled, walked)

B – that winter morning, juan **whistled** as he walked across the playground to the school building

C – That winter morning, Juan **whistled** as he walked across the playground to the school building.

81. **trudged**

PARAGRAPH – new topic
TYPES OF SENTENCES – complex; simple
COMMA – subordinate clause at beginning of complex sentence
VERB TENSE – "was" is past tense of irregular verb "to be"
SPELLING RULE – homophones (new/knew/gnu)
OTHER SKILLS – strong verb practice

B – as he **trudged** to school with his heavy burden juan was happy. he couldn't wait to share his mexican custom with his new friends

C –   As he **trudged** to school with his heavy burden, Juan was happy. He couldn't wait to share his Mexican custom with his new friends.

82. **anticipated**

NO PARAGRAPH – concluding sentence
TYPE OF SENTENCE – complex (subordinate clause at beginning)
COMMA – transition; subordinate clause at beginning; noun list
VERB TENSE – add "ed" to end of regular verbs to put in past tense
SPELLING RULE – "i" before "e"
OTHER SKILLS – strong verb practice; discuss use of adverbs and adverbial phrases—adverbs of more than one word (happily, at school, that evening, with his family); noun (Juan) needed for clarity (students use too many pronouns)

B – finally because it was december 16ᵗʰ he happily **anticipated** the day at school and then going home that evening to celebrate Posada with his family relatives and mexican neighbors.

C – Finally, because it was December 16ᵗʰ, Juan happily **anticipated** the day at school and then going home that evening to celebrate Posada with his family, relatives, and Mexican neighbors.

83. **surrounded, lugged**

PARAGRAPH – new action
TYPES OF SENTENCES – both simple
COMMA – introductory adverb
VERB TENSE – add "ed" to end of regular verbs to put in past tense
OTHER SKILLS – hyphen bet. 2 words acting as 1; strong verb practice; "that" refers only to things; go over ordinal numbers (first, second, third, fourth, fifth, etc.)
LITERARY DEVICE – suspense

B – suddenly big fifth graders **surrounded** juan. they wanted to know what was in the box that he **lugged** in his arms

C –   Suddenly, big fifth-graders **surrounded** Juan. They wanted to know what was in the box that he **lugged** in his arms.

84. panicked, croaked, precious

PARAGRAPH – shift to new subject

TYPES OF SENTENCES – all three simple

VERB TENSE – add "ed" to end of regular verbs to put in past tense; "had learned" is pluperfect tense to indicate action that took place before this paragraph; "had" is past tense of irregular verb "to have"

OTHER SKILL – strong verb practice

LITERARY DEVICE – suspense

B – juan **panicked**. he forgot all the english he had learned. his voice **croaked** in fear of losing all the **precious** things he had in his box

C –   Juan **panicked**. He forgot all the English he had learned. His voice **croaked** in fear of losing all the **precious** things he had in his box.

> **NOTE:** *If you think your students can handle correcting a run-on sentence, remove all the periods and insert "and" instead. Warn them about the run-on sentence. You can do this whenever there are several simple sentences in a Caught'ya. Run-on sentences are the bane of student writing at any level!*

---

85. squeaked, attempted, evade

PARAGRAPH – new person speaking (quotation)

TYPE OF SENTENCE – complex (with simple sentence quotes)

CAPITALIZATION – always capitalize the first letter of a quote unless it is a continuation

PUNCTUATION – use of quotation marks around what is said out loud; question marks needed for questions in quote

VERB TENSE – add "ed" to end of regular verbs to put in past tense; switch to present tense for quote (in Spanish)

SPELLING RULES – consonant/vowel/consonant + suffix = double 2nd consonant (bigger)

OTHER SKILLS – strong verb practice; comparisons (big/bigger/biggest); use of too many adjectives for clarity—noun is necessary

LITERARY DEVICE – suspense

B – déjame solo. basta, he **squeaked** out as he **attempted** to **evade** the bigger boys by running into the school

C –   "Déjame solo. Basta," he **squeaked** out as he **attempted** to **evade** the bigger boys by running into the school. (*Dayhamay so-low. Bahstah = Leave me alone. Enough.*)

86. safeguard

PARAGRAPH – narrator comment

TYPES OF SENTENCES – simple; compound

PUNCTUATION – use of quotation marks around foreign word not known in English

COMMA – compound sentence

VERB TENSE – "should have" needs to be used as a hypothetical case ("should of," which students like to use, is incorrect and does not make sense)

SPELLING RULE – homophones (to, too, two)

CONTRACTION – didn't = did not

OTHER SKILLS – review FANBOYS (See Caught'ya #9); review prepositions

B – juan should have asked his father to walk him too school to **safeguard** the "golosinas. he should of spoken in english but he didnt

C – Juan should have asked his father to walk him to school to **safeguard** the "golosinas." He should have spoken in English, but he did not. (**goloseenahs—accent on "see"**)

87. discern

PARAGRAPH – back to fifth-graders

TYPES OF SENTENCES – both simple

VERB TENSE – "did" is past tense of irregular verb "to do"; use of pluperfect (had spoken) to denote action that took place before this paragraph

SPELLING RULES – homophones (know/no and new/gnu/knew); consonant/vowel/consonant + suffix = double 2nd consonant (bigger)

OTHER SKILLS – comparatives (big/bigger/biggest); hyphen between 2 words acting as 1; negatives

B – the bigger fifth graders did not no that juan was knew in this country. they did not **discern** that he had spoken in spanish

C – The bigger fifth-graders did not know that Juan was new in this country. They did not **discern** that he had spoken in Spanish.

88. rowdy, bullies, insulted

No paragraph – continuation

Types of sentences – both simple

Punctuation – use of quotation marks around words that were supposedly said out loud

Comma – two adjectives not separated by "and" where 2nd adj. is not age, color, or linked to noun

Verb tense – add "ed" to end of regular verbs to put in past tense; "thought" is past tense of irregular verb "to think"; need for pluperfect (had insulted) to denote action that took place before this paragraph

Spelling – homophones (there/their/they're)

Other skills – strong verb practice; avoiding direct quotes by inserting "that"; use of hyphen for two words acting as one adjective

B – the fifth-grade **rowdy bullies** thought that juan had **insulted** them. they thought that he had called them "dookies and a nasty word that **insulted** there mothers

C – The fifth-grade, **rowdy bullies** thought that Juan had **insulted** them. They thought that he had called them "dookies" and a nasty word that **insulted** their mothers.

> **NOTE:** *This and the following Caught'ya are other good places to practice run-on sentences if you wish.*

---

89. irate

No paragraph – same topic

Types of sentences – both simple

Verb tense – add "ed" to end of regular verbs to put in past tense; "made" is past tense of irregular verb "to make"

Spelling rule – compound word

Other skills – strong verbs; hyphen between 2 wds. acting as 1; review ordinal numbers (first, second, etc.)

Literary device – building suspense

B – this made the angry fifth graders even more **irate**. they chased juan all the way to his classroom

C – This made the angry fifth-graders even more **irate**. They chased Juan all the way to his classroom.

90. fracas, sped

PARAGRAPH – new person speaking

TYPE OF SENTENCE – complex (subordinate clause with compound verb at the end)

CAPITALIZATION – always capitalize the first letter of a quote unless it is a continuation

PUNCTUATION – quotation marks around what is said out loud; question mark needed after quote that is a question

COMMA – introductory word

VERB TENSE – switch to present tense for quote; add "ed" to end of regular verbs to put in past tense; "stood" is past tense of irregular verb "to stand"; "sped" is past tense of irregular verb "to speed"

SPELLING RULES – compound word; consonant/vowel/consonant + suffix = double second consonant (grabbed)

PLURAL VS. POSSESSIVE – possessive of singular noun

B – well what is this **fracas** asked juans teacher as she stood in the doorway to the room and grabbed juan as he **sped** past her

C – "Well, what is this **fracas**?" asked Juan's teacher as she stood in the doorway to the room and grabbed Juan as he **sped** past her.

91. ruffians

NO PARAGRAPH – same person speaking; Paragraph – new person speaking

TYPES OF SENTENCES – both simple quotes

CAPITALIZATION – always capitalize the first letter of a quote unless it is a continuation

PUNCTUATION – use of quotation marks around what is said out loud

COMMAS – introductory word; after quote that is not a question

VERB TENSE – switch to present tense for quote; add "ed" to end of regular verbs to put in past tense; "said" is past tense of verb "to say"

SPELLING RULES – homophones (won/one)

CONTRACTION – Ma'am = Madam

OTHER SKILLS – strong verb practice; review simple possessive pronouns; hyphen between 2 words acting as 1

LITERARY DEVICE – conversation

B – are you **ruffians** picking on one of my third graders she continued. no ma'am said won of the fifth graders

C – "Are you **ruffians** picking on one of my third-graders?" she continued.
"No, Ma'am," said one of the fifth-graders.

92. insulted, blurted

PARAGRAPH – new person speaking

TYPE OF SENTENCE – simple quote

CAPITALIZATION – always capitalize the first letter of a quote unless it is a continuation

PUNCTUATION – use of quotation marks around what is said out loud

COMMA – end of quote that is not a question or exclamation

VERB TENSE – add "ed" to end of regular verbs to put in past tense; note use of past tense in quote to indicate something that happened prior to this paragraph

SPELLING RULE – if form plural of nouns that end in consonant "y" by replacing "y" with "ies"

OTHER SKILL – strong verb practice

B – he **insulted** us **blurted** out another of the bullies

C – "He **insulted** us," **blurted** out another of the bullies.

---

93. intentionally

PARAGRAPH – new person speaking

TYPES OF SENTENCES – both simple (second has compound verb)

CAPITALIZATION – always capitalize the first letter of a quote unless it is a continuation; always capitalize "I"

PUNCTUATION – use of quotation marks around what is said out loud

COMMAS – end of quote that is not a question or exclamation; direct address

VERB TENSE – switch to present tense for quote; "said" is past tense of irregular verb "to say"

PLURAL VS. POSSESSIVE – possessive of singular noun

CONTRACTION – don't = do not

OTHER SKILL – strong verb practice

B – i don't think juan would do that **intentionally** said the juans teacher. go to class boys and leave my students alone

C – "I don't think Juan would do that **intentionally**," said the Juan's teacher. "Go to class, boys, and leave my students alone."

94. dreadful, stare, critter

PARAGRAPH – new person speaking

TYPE OF SENTENCE – simple quote

CAPITALIZATION – always capitalize the first letter of a quote unless it is a continuation

PUNCTUATION – use of quotation marks around what is said out loud

COMMAS – before quote; direct address with repeated word

VERB TENSE – add "ed" to end of regular verbs to put in past tense; "was" is past tense of irregular verb "to be"; switch to present tense for quote

SPELLING RULES – consonant/vowel/consonant + suffix = double 2nd consonant (biggest); homophones (know/no)

CONTRACTION – we're = we are

OTHER SKILLS – comparatives (big/bigger/biggest); hyphen between 2 words acting as 1

LITERARY DEVICES – building suspense again; anadiplosis

B – the biggest fifth grader gave juan a **dreadful stare** that said were not finished with you you little **critter**

C – The biggest fifth-grader gave Juan a **dreadful stare** that said, "We're not finished with you, you little **critter**."

95. apprehensive

PARAGRAPH – new subject

TYPES OF SENTENCES – both simple

COMMAS – always put commas around "too" if it means "also"

VERB TENSE – "was" and "were" are past tense of irregular verb "to be"

SPELLING RULES – compound word; homophones (to/too/two)

OTHER SKILL – review simple possessive pronouns

LITERARY DEVICE – building suspense

B – juan was scared. his classmates were **apprehensive** to

C – Juan was scared. His classmates were **apprehensive**, too.

96. bullied

NO PARAGRAPH – same subject; continuation

TYPE OF SENTENCE – complex

VERB TENSE – note use of pluperfect (had bullied) to refer to action that took place prior to this paragraph; "was" is past tense of irregular verb "to be"

SPELLING RULE – compound word

OTHER SKILLS – comparative (big/bigger/biggest); hyphen between 2 words acting as 1; negative

B – the big fifth graders had **bullied** them before whenever a teacher was not around

C – The big fifth-graders had **bullied** them before whenever a teacher was not around.

97. consumed, victims

No paragraph – same topic

Type of sentence – compound

Commas – introductory adverb; compound sentence

Verb tense – add "ed" to end of regular verbs to put in past tense; "took" is past tense of irregular verb "to take"

Spelling rules – consonant/vowel/consonant + suffix = double 2nd consonant (bigger); form plural of nouns that end in consonant "y" by replacing "y" with "ies" (goodies/ cookies); homophones (right/write/rite); plural of noun that does not end in "s" (children); plurals of words ending in "ch"

Plural vs. possessive – possessive of plural noun

Other skills – strong verb practice; comparatives (big/bigger/biggest); note hyphen in "third-graders'" because of two words acting as one adjective; review FANBOYS

B – sometimes some of the bigger children took the best goodies and all the cookies from third-graders lunches and they **consumed** them write in front of the **victims**

C – Sometimes, some of the bigger children took the best goodies and all the cookies from third-graders' lunches, and they **consumed** them right in front of the **victims**.

---

98. whimpered

Paragraph – new person speaking (quotation)

Type of sentence – complex

Capitalization – always capitalize the first letter of a quote unless it is a continuation

Punctuation – use of quotation marks around what is said out loud; need for question mark at end of quote that is a question

Commas – no commas needed after "friend" since she probably has many friends and thus the name is necessary; unnecessary, extra information (restrictive vs. non-restrictive modifiers for you English buffs)

Verb tense – add "ed" to end of regular verbs to put in past tense; switch to present tense for quote

Spelling rule – "i" before "e" (friend)

Other skills – strong verb practice; review prepositions

B – what can we do **whimpered** _____ to her freind _____ as the teacher closed the door of the classroom behind juan

C – "What can we do?" **whimpered** _____ to her friend _____ as the teacher closed the door of the classroom behind Juan.

99. whispered

PARAGRAPH – new person speaking
TYPE OF SENTENCE – complex
CAPITALIZATION – always capitalize the first letter of a quote unless it is a continuation
PUNCTUATION – use of quotation marks around what is said out loud
COMMA – end of quote that is not a question or exclamation
VERB TENSE – future tense (will come); "could" is past tense of verb "can"
SPELLING RULE – homophones (here/hear)
OTHER SKILLS – strong verb practice; negative; review adverb use

B – those big kids really will come after us now **whispered** _____ quietly so that the teacher could not hear

C – "Those big kids really will come after us now," **whispered** _____ quietly so that the teacher could not hear.

100. agitated

PARAGRAPH – new topic; narrator now speaking
TYPE OF SENTENCE – compound
COMMA – compound sentence
VERB TENSE – add "ed" to end of regular verbs to put in past tense; "became" is past tense of irregular verb "to become"; "were" is past tense of verb "to be"
SPELLING RULES – often confused words (quit/quiet/quite); plural of noun that does not end in "s"; form plural of nouns that end in consonant "y" by replacing "y" with "ies" (bullies); homophones (their/there/they're)
OTHER SKILLS – review simple object pronouns (me, you, him, her, us, them); review FANBOYS

B – the children became quiet as the teacher began class but most of them were **agitated** by there fear of the bullies

C – The children became quiet as the teacher began class, but most of them were **agitated** by their fear of the bullies.

101. apprehensively

PARAGRAPH – new subject
TYPES OF SENTENCES – simple with long introductory participial phrase
COMMAS – participial phrase
VERB TENSE – "went" is past tense of irregular verb "to go"
SPELLING RULES – compound word
PLURAL VS. POSSESSIVE – possessive of singular noun
OTHER SKILLS – "good" is adjective and "well" is adverb; review adverbs; note hyphen in third-grade as it is two words acting as one adjective

B – except for a student occasionally looking **apprehensively** out the doorway the rest of the day went very good in _____s third-grade class

C – Except for a student occasionally looking **apprehensively** out the doorway, the rest of the day went very well in _____'s third-grade class.

102. tradition, procession

PARAGRAPH – new subject

TYPES OF SENTENCES – compound; compound complex (sub. clause at end)

COMMAS – compound sentences; sub. clause at end = no comma

VERB TENSE – add "ed" to end of regular verbs to put in past tense

SPELLING RULE – most nouns form plurals by adding "s"

PLURAL VS. POSSESSIVE – possessive of singular noun

OTHER SKILLS – strong verb practice; collective nouns and pronouns need singular verbs and referents (i.e., never use "their" with pronoun "everyone"); go over simple possessive pronouns; review FANBOYS

B – everyone enjoyed their treats and the class heard all about the mexican **tradition** of Posada. juan explained that he was going to play the part of joseph in the **procession** and he even would wear a beard when he knocked on a neighbors door that evening

C – Everyone enjoyed his or her treats, and the class heard all about the Mexican **tradition** of Posada. Juan explained that he was going to play the part of Joseph in the **procession**, and he even would wear a beard when he knocked on a neighbor's door that evening.

---

103. threatened, wary

NO PARAGRAPH – same focus (students' day)

TYPES OF SENTENCES – complex; compound

COMMA – compound sentence

VERB TENSE – add "ed" to end of regular verbs to put in past tense; "was" is past tense of irregular verb "to be"

SPELLING RULE – homophones (no/know)

OTHER SKILLS – review FANBOYS; hyphen between 2 words acting as 1

B – even after school nothing happened because the teacher walked everyone out. no third graders were **threatened** that day but they were still **wary**

C – Even after school nothing happened because the teacher walked everyone out. No third-graders were **threatened** that day, but they were still **wary**.

---

104. predicament

> **NOTE:** *This is another good Caught'ya to practice run-on sentences if you wish.*

PARAGRAPH – new topic

TYPES OF SENTENCES – complex; simple

COMMA – subordinate clause at beginning of complex sentence

VERB TENSE – add "ed" to end of regular verbs to put in past tense; "had" is past tense of irregular verb "to have"

SPELLING RULES – homophones (whole/hole); often misspelled word (since)

B – juan decided that since this hole mess had been his fault he wanted to fix the **predicament**. he had a plan

C – Juan decided that since this whole mess had been his fault, he wanted to fix the **predicament**. He had a plan.

105. peers

N0 PARAGRAPH – same topic

TYPE OF SENTENCE – complex

COMMA – subordinate clause at beginning of complex sentence

VERB TENSE – add "ed" to end of regular verbs to put in past tense; "told" is past tense of irregular verb "to tell"

Plural vs. possessive – possessive of singular noun

OTHER SKILLS – strong verb practice; better to change word so you don't use the same word twice in a sentence (change one instance of "plan" to "idea")

B – when juan told his plan to his **peers** marie and the others offered to help put juans plan into action

C – When Juan told his plan to his **peers**, Marie and the others offered to help put Juan's idea into action.

---

106. relatives

PARAGRAPH – new person speaking and new time

TYPES OF SENTENCES – simple (compound verb); simple quote

CAPITALIZATION – always capitalize the first letter of a quote unless it is a continuation

PUNCTUATION – quotation marks around what is said out loud; quotes around word referred to in context (yes)

COMMAS – introductory adverb; before quote; after quote; extra information (explanation); no comma after "meant" as it is an indirect quote

VERB TENSE – add "ed" to end of regular verbs to put in past tense; "said" is past tense of irregular verb "to say"; "meant" is past tense of the verb "to mean"

SPELLING RULE – homophones (their/there/they're)

OTHER SKILLS – strong verb practice; comparatives; go over adjectives (this, that, these, and those)

B – that night juan and marie called they're relatives in mexico and in france and asked a big favor. their **relatives** said sí and oui both of which meant yes

C – 	That night, Juan and Marie called their relatives in Mexico and in France and asked a big favor. Their **relatives** said, "Sí," and "Oui," both of which meant "Yes." (***See; Wee***)

107. ongoing, dilemma

2 Paragraphs – new person enters and then new person speaking
Types of sentences – simple; simple quote
Capitalization – always capitalize the first letter of a quote unless it is a continuation
Punctuation – use of quotation marks around what is said out loud
Commas – appositive (extra information about a noun); put commas around "too" if it means "also"; before quote
Verb tense – add "ed" to end of regular verbs to put in past tense; "said" is past tense of irregular verb "to say"
Spelling rule – homophones (to/too/two and their/there/they're)
Other skills – strong verbs; hyphen in 2 wds. acting as 1; collective noun "class" needs singular verb and referents
Literary device – building of mystery

B – the class explained the **ongoing dilemma** with the fifth graders and asked the help of their teacher
_____. she too said yes

C – The class explained the **ongoing dilemma** with the fifth-graders and asked the help of their teacher,
_____.

She, too, said, "Yes."

---

108. toiled

Paragraph – new time
Types of sentences – both simple (compound verb in first sentence)
Punctuation – quotation marks around foreign word
Commas – long introductory adverb; verb series
Verb tense – add "ed" to end of regular verbs to put in past tense
Spelling rule – consonant/vowel/consonant + suffix = double 2nd consonant (planned)
Plural vs. possessive – possessive of singular noun
Other skills – strong verbs; write out numbers to 121; hyphen needed in two words acting as one adjective

B – for the next 3 weeks _____ s third-grade class planned prepared **toiled** and worked. juans mother ordered goodies from the local mexican "panadería

C – For the next three weeks, _____'s third-grade class planned, prepared, **toiled**, and worked. Juan's mother ordered goodies from the local Mexican "panadería." (**pahnahdayreeyah— accent on the "ree"**)

109. occasionally, glared

No paragraph – same time

Type of sentence – compound

Commas – long introductory adverb; compound sentence

Verb tense – add "ed" to end of regular verbs to put in past tense

Spelling rule – form plural of nouns that end in consonant "y" by replacing "y" with "ies" (bullies)

Plural vs. possessive – possessive of singular noun

Other skills – strong verb practice; write out numbers to 121; hyphen between 2 words acting as 1; use "like" only to compare two nouns (or pronouns) directly (i.e., Dogs are *like* cats in many ways.); review adverbs; review FANBOYS

Literary device – building of suspense

B – for those three weeks the bullies **occasionally** snatched a cookie from a third-graders lunch box or teased other students but they always **glared** at juan as if they wanted to beat him up

C – For those three weeks, the bullies **occasionally** snatched a cookie from a third-grader's lunch box or teased other students, but they always **glared** at Juan as if they wanted to beat him up.

110. implied, threat

No paragraph – same topic

Type of sentence – complex

Commas – interrupter

Verb tense – "could" is past tense of irregular verb "can"; "hung" is past tense of verb "to hang"

Spelling rules – form plural of nouns that end in consonant "y" by replacing "y" with "ies" (bullies); homophones (their/there/they're)

Other skills – negative; never split verb parts nor infinitives; comparatives (large/larger/largest); hyphen between 2 words acting as 1

B – the larger bullies could never carry out there **implied threat** however because all the other third-graders hung around juan all the time

C – The larger bullies never could carry out their **implied threat**, however, because all the other third-graders hung around Juan all the time.

111. unaccompanied, whenever

No paragraph – same topic

Types of sentences – simple; complex

Verb tense – "was" and "were" are past tense of irregular verb "to be"

Spelling rules – homophones (their/there/they're); compound words

Other skills – write out numbers to 121; hyphen in between two words acting as one adjective

B – juan was never **unaccompanied** at school. they're were always at least 10 other third-grade students around him **whenever** he was out of the classroom

C – Juan was never **unaccompanied** at school. There were always at least ten other third-grade students around him **whenever** he was out of the classroom.

112. drafted, via

PARAGRAPH – new time

TYPES OF SENTENCES – simple; simple (compound verb)

COMMA – introductory adverb (optional here)

VERB TENSE – add "ed" to end of regular verbs to put in past tense; "was" is past tense of irregular verb "to be"; "sent" is past tense of verb "to send"

SPELLING RULE – homophones (their/they're/there and write/rite/right)

OTHER SKILLS – no hyphen needed in "third grade" since it is a noun; hyphen needed in "fifth-grade" since together the 2 words are 1 adjective

B – finally everything was ready. the third grade **drafted** a letter to the fifth-grade students and sent it **via** their teacher who helped them write it

C –   Finally, everything was ready. The third grade **drafted** a letter to the fifth-grade students and sent it **via** their teacher who helped them write it.

---

113. misunderstanding, foreign

> **NOTE:** *This is a longer Caught'ya due to its nature as a letter. You may want to spend an hour on it followed by a brief, end-of-the-year letter-writing unit and have students exchange letters or write a letter to himself/herself. You could collect these letters, save them, and return them to the students when they leave your school. Emphasize elaboration and correct letter-writing format. Middle-school teachers beg you to make sure that students learn not to indent the greeting. For some reason, children arrive in middle school with this incorrect habit ingrained in their minds. It really is hard to break them of it.*

2 PARAGRAPHS – letter beginning (do not indent greeting); new topic

TYPES OF SENTENCES – simple; compound; simple (compound verb); simple; simple; simple

CAPITALIZATION – capitalize every word in greeting; capitalize only the first word in closing; rules for normal capitalization of proper noun apply to headings and signatures

COMMAS – between city and state; in date; after greeting in friendly letter; appositive (more information about a noun, Juan); compound sentence; after closing of letter

VERB TENSE – switch to present tense for invitation which is technically a quote

SPELLING RULES – homophones (its/it's); compound words; form plural of nouns that end in consonant "y" by replacing "y" with "ies" (cookies); difficult word (o'clock)

PLURAL VS. POSSESSIVE – possessive of singular noun

OTHER SKILLS – letter-writing format; do not begin a sentence with FANBOYS (conjunction); write out numbers to 121; abbreviation "p.m."; hyphen between 2 words acting as 1

LITERARY DEVICE – letter within story

B –

           _____ elementary school
           [*your school's address*]
           [*your city*], [*your state*] [*your zip code*]

           may ____ _____ (*put the correct date*)

the fifth-grade class
_____ elementary school
[*your school's address*]
[*your city*], [*your state*] [*your zip code*]

dear fifth graders

we apologize for the **misunderstanding** you had with juan one of our two new **foreign** students. we know that some of you have been mean to us in the past but maybe its because you like our cookies. so we invite you to a party to let you meet juan and marie and to share some really yummy mexican and french goodies with us please come to our classroom friday at 2 o'clock p m. we want to get to know you too. we also want to know what it is like to be a big fifth grader

sincerely yours

_____ s third-grade class

C –

           _____ Elementary School
           [*your school's address*]
           [*your city*], [*your state*] [*your zip code*]

           May ____, _____ (*put the correct date*)

The Fifth-grade Class
_____ Elementary School
[*your school's address*]
[*your city*], [*your state*] [*your zip code*]

Dear Fifth-Graders,

    We apologize for the **misunderstanding** you had with Juan, one of our two new **foreign** students. We know that some of you have been mean to us in the past, but maybe it's because you like our cookies. We invite you to a party to let you meet Juan and Marie and to share some really yummy Mexican and French goodies with us.

    Please come to our classroom Friday at two o'clock p.m. We want to get to know you, too. We also want to know what it is like to be a big fifth-grader.

    Sincerely yours,
    _____ 's Third-grade Class

114. epistle

PARAGRAPH – new time

TYPE OF SENTENCE – simple

COMMAS – introductory adverb (optional)

VERB TENSE – add "ed" to end of regular verbs to put in past tense

SPELLING RULES – "i" before "e"; homophones (their/they're/there)

PLURAL VS. POSSESSIVE – possessive of singular noun

OTHER SKILLS – strong verb practice; hyphen needed between two words acting as one adjective

B – the next day _____ s third-grade class received a reply to their **epistle**

C – The next day, _____'s third-grade class received a reply to their **epistle**.

115. accept, invitation

PARAGRAPH – letter beginning (do not indent greeting)

TYPES OF SENTENCES – all simple

CAPITALIZATION – capitalize every word in greeting; capitalize only the first word in closing; rules for normal capitalization of proper noun apply to headings and signatures

PUNCTUATION – question mark needed in question

COMMAS – between city and state; in date; after greeting in friendly letter; two adjectives not separated by "and" where 2nd is not age, color, or linked to noun; after closing of letter

VERB TENSE – switch to future tense for acceptance of invitation which is technically a quote

SPELLING RULES – homophones (its/it's); form plural of nouns that end in consonant "y" by replacing "y" with "ies" (cookies); difficult word (o'clock)

PLURAL VS. POSSESSIVE – possessive of singular noun

CONJUNCTION – we'll = we will

OTHER SKILLS – letter-writing format; often-confused words (accept vs. except); write out numbers to 121; abbreviation "p.m."; use of parentheses for nickname; hyphen needed when two words are acting as one adjective

LITERARY DEVICE – letter within story

B –

_____ elementary school
[*your school's address*]
[*your city*], [*your state*] [*your zip code*]

may ____ _____ (*put the correct date*)

the third-grade class
_____ elementary school
[*your school's address*]
[*your city*], [*your state*] [*your zip code*]

dear third graders

we will **accept** your **invitation**. its a nice fun surprise for us. well come to your classroom friday at 2 o'clock p.m. did you say cookies

_____s fifth grade class
(the cookie monsters)

C –

_____ Elementary School
[*your school's address*]
[*your city*], [*your state*] [*your zip code*]

May ____, _____ (*put the correct date*)

The Third-grade Class
_____ Elementary School
[*your school's address*]
[*your city*], [*your state*] [*your zip code*]

Dear Third-Graders,

We will **accept** your **invitation**. It's a nice, fun surprise for us. We'll come to your classroom Friday at two o'clock p.m. Did you say cookies?

_____'s Fifth-grade Class
(the Cookie Monsters)

NOTE: *This is a longer Caught'ya. Plan to spend at least an hour on it. You may want to have your students write a letter to the fourth-graders at your school asking them what it will be like next year in the fourth grade. Again, emphasize elaboration as well as not indenting the greeting.*

116. parcel

PARAGRAPH – new time

TYPES OF SENTENCES – all simple

VERB TENSE – add "ed" to end of regular verbs to put in past tense; "came" is past tense of irregular verb "to come"

SPELLING RULE – often misspelled word (finally)

PLURAL VS. POSSESSIVE – possessive of singular noun

OTHER SKILLS – strong verb practice; collective pronoun requires singular verb and referents (like possessive pronouns); need for hyphen between 2 words acting as 1 adjective; subject-verb agreement ("each student" is singular and thus you cannot use "their" which is plural)

B – friday finally arrived. everyone in _____ s third-grade class came in early. each student carried their **parcel**

C – Friday finally arrived. Everyone in _____'s third-grade class came in early. Each student carried a **parcel**.

---

117. awesome

NO PARAGRAPH – same topic (detail)

TYPE OF SENTENCE – simple (compound verb)

CAPITALIZATION – do not capitalize the names of subjects unless they are the name of a language (English, French, Spanish)

COMMAS – interrupter of extra information; noun series within interrupter

VERB TENSE – add "ed" to end of regular verbs to put in past tense

OTHER SKILLS – strong verb practice; collective noun (class) takes singular verb

B – all day long instead of math science social studies and language arts the class practiced greetings in french and spanish and prepared for the **awesome** party

C – All day long, instead of math, science, social studies, and language arts, the class practiced greetings in French and Spanish and prepared for the **awesome** party.

---

118. precisely

PARAGRAPH – new time

TYPES OF SENTENCES – simple (compound subject); simple

COMMA – long introductory adverb

VERB TENSE – add "ed" to end of regular verbs to put in past tense; "was" is past tense of irregular verb "to be"

SPELLING RULES – homophones (their/there/they're); difficult word (o'clock)

OTHER SKILLS – write out numbers to 121; review adverbs; hyphen between 2 words acting as 1; review subject and object pronouns (the error in this one should be obvious to your students)

LITERARY DEVICE – suspense building

B – At two o'clock **precisely** the fifth graders and theyre teacher arrived at the door. Everything was ready for they

C – At two o'clock **precisely**, the fifth-graders and their teacher arrived at the door. Everything was ready for them.

119. guests

Paragraph – new action with new people speaking

Type of sentence – complex (subordinate clause at beginning)

Capitalization – always capitalize the first letter of a quote unless it is a continuation

Punctuation – use of quotation marks around what is said out loud

Commas – subordinate clause at beginning; noun series; no comma after "of" and "and" since these are indirect quotes

Verb tense – add "ed" to end of regular verbs to put in past tense

Spelling rules – compound word; homophones (their/there/they're); form plural of nouns that end in consonant "y" by replacing "y" with "ies" (cries)

Other skills – strong verb practice; hyphen between 2 words acting as 1

B – as they opened the door of the classroom juan marie and all the third-graders greeted there **guests** with cries of bienvenue and hola

C –   As they opened the door of the classroom, Juan, Marie, and all the third-graders greeted their **guests** with cries of "Bienvenue" and "Hola." (***Beeahnvenoo—don't pronounce the first "n," stress the last syllable, and the "noo" rhymes with "moo"; Ohla.***)

---

120. decorated, confections, perched, decoratively

No paragraph – same topic

Types of sentences – simple (compound subject); simple (compound subject); simple (compound verb)

Commas – noun series

Verb tense – add "ed" to end of regular verbs to put in past tense; "had" is past tense of irregular verb "to have"; "were" is past tense of "to be"

Spelling rules – most nouns form plurals by adding "s"

Plural vs. possessive – possessive of singular nouns

Other skills – strong-verb practice

Literary device – strong-verb description

B – pictures flags and posters of france and mexico **decorated** the room. hundreds of mexican and french **confections perched decoratively** on the desks. they had come from france and mexico or had been made according to the recipes of maries and juans relatives

C – Pictures, flags, and posters of France and Mexico **decorated** the room. Hundreds of Mexican and French **confections perched decoratively** on the desks. They had come from France and Mexico or had been made according to the recipes of Marie's and Juan's relatives.

121. transported, directly

No paragraph – same topic

Type of sentence – simple

Capitalization – capitalize the names of countries

Punctuation – exclamation mark needed for emphasis

Verb tense – add "ed" to end of regular verbs to put in past tense; "had been" is pluperfect of the verb "to have" and is needed here to refer to action that took place before this paragraph

Other skills – use "as if" and not "like" because "like" directly compares only two nouns or pronouns (use "as if" if a verb is involved); strong verb use

Literary devices – description; simile with "as"

B – the room looked like it had been **transported directly** from france and mexico

C – The room looked as if it had been **transported directly** from France and Mexico!

---

122. astonished, delighted, confections

Paragraph – new subject (now talking about fifth-graders)

Types of sentences – simple (compound object); simple

Verb tense – "were" is past tense of irregular verb "to be"; "ate" is past tense of verb "to eat"

Spelling rule – often confused words (were/we're)

Other skills – review ordinal numbers (first, second, etc.); hyphen between 2 words acting as 1; review simple subject pronouns (I, you, he, she, we, they)

B – the fifth graders were **astonished** and **delighted**. they ate the **confections**

C –   The fifth-graders were **astonished** and **delighted**. They ate the **confections**.

---

123. established, friendships

No paragraph – same topic

Type of sentence – compound

Commas – compound sentence; two adjectives not separated by "and" where second adjective is not age, color, or linked to noun

Verb tense – add "ed" to end of regular verbs to put in past tense

Spelling rules – homophones (gnu/new/knew)

Other skills – hyphen between 2 words acting as 1; strong verb practice; too many pronouns for clarity (substitute noun for first instance of pronoun "they"); review ordinal numbers; comparatives (young/younger/youngest and small/smaller/smallest); review FANBOYS

B – they learned to sing songs in french and spanish and they **established** gnu **friendships** with the younger smaller students

C – The fifth-graders learned to sing songs in French and Spanish, and they **established** new **friendships** with the younger, smaller students.

124. misdeeds, mistreat

No paragraph – same topic (detail)

Type of sentence – simple (compound verb)

Verb tense – add "ed" to end of regular verbs to put in past tense

Spelling rule – homophones (their/there/they're and to/too/two)

Other skills – strong verb practice; do not begin a sentence with a conjunction (FANBOYS); too many pronouns for clarity (substitute noun for first instance of "they"); review ordinal numbers; hyphen between 2 words acting as 1

B – and they apologized for there past **misdeeds** and promised never too **mistreat** third graders again

C – The fifth-graders apologized for their past **misdeeds** and promised never to **mistreat** third-graders again.

125. mischievous, entirely

Paragraph – new topic

Punctuation – use of ellipses to indicate possible future action

Commas – introductory adverb (optional); relative pronoun clause (not necessary info)

Verb tense – "were" is past tense of irregular verb "to be"

Other skills – review ordinal numbers; review adjectives and adverbs; relative pronouns "who" and "whom" ("who" is subject, and "whom" is the object); hyphen between 2 words acting as 1

Literary device – leave your reader hanging

B – now the fourth graders who were a **mischievous** group were another matter **entirely**

C – Now, the fourth-graders, who were a **mischievous** group, were another matter **entirely**...

> **NOTE:** *Now invite your students to write a sequel to the story. What is going to happen to Juan and Marie? Will the friendship among the third- and fifth-graders continue?*

BIBLIOGRAPHY

♥ Resource contains good suggestions for writing

Bescherelle 2: L'orthographe Pour Tous. Paris: Librairie Hatier, 1990.

Caplan, Rebekah and Catherine Keech. *Showing Writing: A Training Program to Help Students Be Specific.* Berkeley, CA: University of California Press, 1980.

Dean, Nancy. *Voice Lessons: Classroom Activities to Teach Diction, Detail, Imagery, Syntax, and Tone.* Gainesville, FL: Maupin House Publishing, 2000.

Dierking, Connie Campbell and Sherra Ann Jones. *Growing Up Writing: Mini-Lessons for Emergent and Beginning Writers.* Gainesville, FL: Maupin House Publishing, 2003. ♥

Elgin, Suzette Haden. "The Great Grammar Myth." National Writing Project Occasional Paper #5. Berkeley, CA: University of California Press, 1982.

Forney, Melissa. *Dynamite Writing Ideas! Empowering Students to Become Authors.* Gainesville, FL: Maupin House Publishing, 1996. ♥

___. *Razzle Dazzle Writing: Achieving Success Through 50 Target Skills.* Gainesville, FL: Maupin House Publishing, 2001. ♥

___. *The Writing Menu: Ensuring Success for Every Student.* Gainesville, FL: Maupin House Publishing, 1999. ♥

Freeman, Marcia S. *Building a Writing Community: A Practical Guide.* Gainesville, FL: Maupin House Publishing, 1995. ♥

___. *Listen to This: Developing an Ear for Expository.* Gainesville, FL: Maupin House Publishing, 1997. ♥

___. *Teaching the Youngest Writers: A Practical Guide.* Gainesville, FL: Maupin House Publishing, 1998. ♥

French Dictionary. Glasgow: HarperCollins, 1988.

Hacker, Diane. *A Writer's Reference (Third Edition).* Boston: Bedford Books, 1995.

Haley-James, Shirley and John Warren Stewig. *Houghton Mifflin English.* Boston: Houghton Mifflin, 1988.

Johnson, Bea. *Never Too Early to Write: Adventures in the K-1 Writing Workshop.* Gainesville, FL: Maupin House Publishing, 1999. ♥

Kiester, Jane. *Blowing Away the State Writing Assessment Test.* Gainesville, FL: Maupin House Publishing, 1996. ♥

___. *Caught'ya! Grammar with a Giggle.* Gainesville, FL: Maupin House Publishing, 1990.

___. *Caught'ya Again! More Grammar with a Giggle.* Gainesville, FL: Maupin House Publishing, 1992. ♥

___. *The Chortling Bard: Grammar with a Giggle for High Schools* Gainesville, FL: Maupin House Publishing, 1997.

___. *Eggbert, the Ball, Bounces by Himself: Caught'ya! Grammar with a Giggle for First Grade.* Gainesville, FL: Maupin House Publishing, 2006.

___. *Elementary, My Dear! Grammar with a Giggle for Grades 1, 2, and 3.* Gainesville, FL: Maupin House Publishing, 2000.

___. *Giggles in the Middle: Caught'ya! Grammar with a Giggle for Middle School.* Gainesville, FL: Maupin House Publishing, 2006.

___. *Putrescent Petra Finds Friends: Caught'ya! Grammar with a Giggle for Second Grade.* Gainesville, FL: Maupin House Publishing, 2006.

Laird, Charlton, preparer. *Webster's New World Thesaurus.* New York: Simon and Schuster, 1985.

Ramondino, Salvatore, ed. *El New World Diccionario Español/Inglés, Inglés/Español,* Segunda Edición. New York: New American Library, 1996.

Sherwin, J. Stephen. *Four Problems in Teaching English: A Critique of Research.* Scranton, PA: International Textbook Company, 1969.

Sitton, Rebecca and Robert Forest. *Quick-Word Handbook for Beginning Writers.* North Billerica, MA: Curriculum Associates, 1994. ♥

___. *Quick-Word Handbook for Everyday Writers.* North Billerica, MA: Curriculum Associates, 1994. ♥

___. *Quick-Word Handbook for Practical Writing.* North Billerica, MA: Curriculum Associates, 1994.

Stein, Jess, ed. *The Random House Dictionary of the English Language (Unabridged Edition).* New York: Random House, 1967.

Warriner, John, and Sheila Laws Graham. *Warriner's English Grammar and Composition, Complete Course.* New York: Harcourt Brace Jovanovich, 1957.

___. *Warriner's English Grammar and Composition, Third Course.* New York: Harcourt Brace Jovanovich, 1977.

Wong, Harry K. and Rosemary T. Wong. The First Days of School: How to Be an Effective Teacher. Mountain View, CA: Harry K. Wong Publications, 1998.